DISCOVER
SHIBORI

CREATIVE TECHNIQUES IN NATURAL INDIGO DYEING

DEBBIE MADDY

stashBOOKS.
an imprint of C&T Publishing

Text and photography copyright © 2024 by Debbie Maddy

Artwork and photography copyright © 2024 by C&T Publishing, Inc.

Publisher: Amy Barrett-Daffin

Creative Director: Gailen Runge

Senior Editor: Roxane Cerda

Technical Editor: Kathryn Patterson

Cover/Book Designer: April Mostek

Production Coordinator: Zinnia Heinzmann

Illustrator: Aliza Shalit

Photography Coordinator: Rachel Ackley

Front cover photography by C&T Publishing

Styled photography by Jodi Foucher, unless otherwise noted

Instructional photography by Debbie Maddy, unless otherwise noted

Published by Stash Books, an imprint of C&T Publishing, Inc., P.O. Box 1456, Lafayette, CA 94549

Attention Teachers: C&T Publishing, Inc., encourages the use of our books as texts for teaching. You can find lesson plans for many of our titles at ctpub.com or contact us at ctinfo@ctpub.com.

We take great care to ensure that the information included in our products is accurate and presented in good faith, but no warranty is provided, nor are results guaranteed. Having no control over the choices of materials or procedures used, neither the author nor C&T Publishing, Inc., shall have any liability to any person or entity with respect to any loss or damage caused directly or indirectly by the information contained in this book. For your convenience, we post an up-to-date listing of corrections on our website (ctpub.com). If a correction is not already noted, please contact our customer service department at ctinfo@ctpub.com or P.O. Box 1456, Lafayette, CA 94549.

Trademark (™) and registered trademark (®) names are used throughout this book. Rather than use the symbols with every occurrence of a trademark or registered trademark name, we are using the names only in the editorial fashion and to the benefit of the owner, with no intention of infringement.

Library of Congress Cataloging-in-Publication Data
Names: Maddy, Debbie, 1950- author.
Title: Discover shibori : creative techniques in natural indigo dyeing / Debbie Maddy.
Description: Lafayette, CA : StashBooks, an imprint of C&T Publishing, [2024] | Summary: "Dive in and learn 35 time-tested Shibori resist dyeing techniques, from making a natural indigo vat to more advanced folding, wrapping, and stitching techniques from around the world. In this book, crafters will master three natural indigo vats then show off their dyed fabrics in six stunning projects"-- Provided by publisher.
Identifiers: LCCN 2024013560 | ISBN 9781644034163 (trade paperback) | ISBN 9781644034170 (ebook)
Subjects: LCSH: Tie-dyeing. | Resist-dyed textiles. | Dyes and dyeing
Classification: LCC TT853.5 .M33 2024 | DDC 746.6/64--dc23/eng/20240430
LC record available at https://lccn.loc.gov/2024013560

Printed in China

10 9 8 7 6 5 4 3 2 1

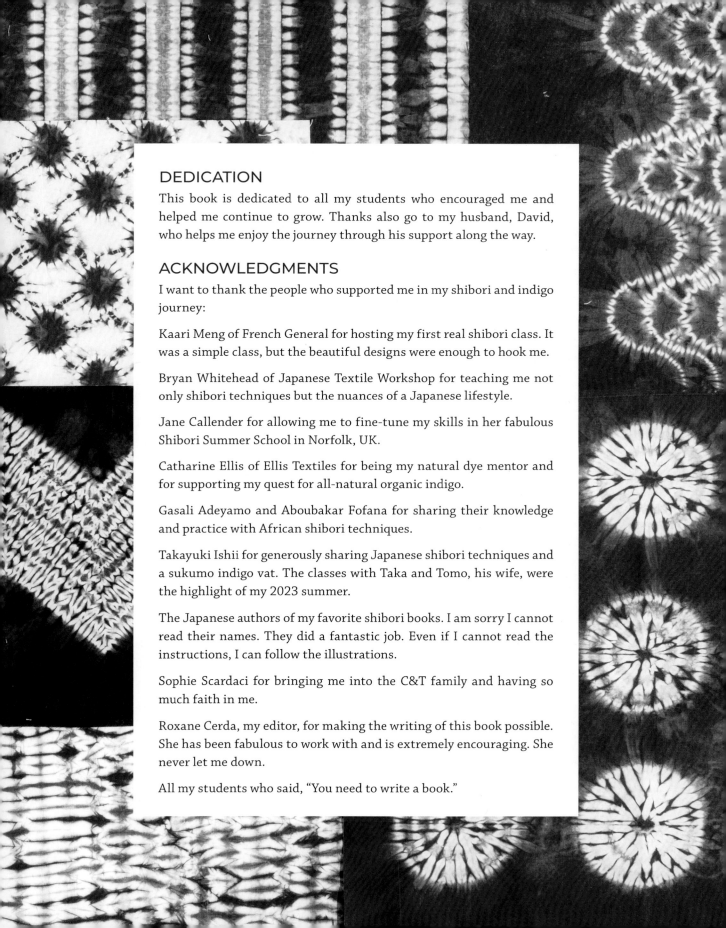

DEDICATION

This book is dedicated to all my students who encouraged me and helped me continue to grow. Thanks also go to my husband, David, who helps me enjoy the journey through his support along the way.

ACKNOWLEDGMENTS

I want to thank the people who supported me in my shibori and indigo journey:

Kaari Meng of French General for hosting my first real shibori class. It was a simple class, but the beautiful designs were enough to hook me.

Bryan Whitehead of Japanese Textile Workshop for teaching me not only shibori techniques but the nuances of a Japanese lifestyle.

Jane Callender for allowing me to fine-tune my skills in her fabulous Shibori Summer School in Norfolk, UK.

Catharine Ellis of Ellis Textiles for being my natural dye mentor and for supporting my quest for all-natural organic indigo.

Gasali Adeyamo and Aboubakar Fofana for sharing their knowledge and practice with African shibori techniques.

Takayuki Ishii for generously sharing Japanese shibori techniques and a sukumo indigo vat. The classes with Taka and Tomo, his wife, were the highlight of my 2023 summer.

The Japanese authors of my favorite shibori books. I am sorry I cannot read their names. They did a fantastic job. Even if I cannot read the instructions, I can follow the illustrations.

Sophie Scardaci for bringing me into the C&T family and having so much faith in me.

Roxane Cerda, my editor, for making the writing of this book possible. She has been fabulous to work with and is extremely encouraging. She never let me down.

All my students who said, "You need to write a book."

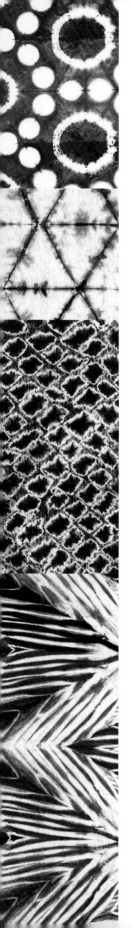

CONTENTS

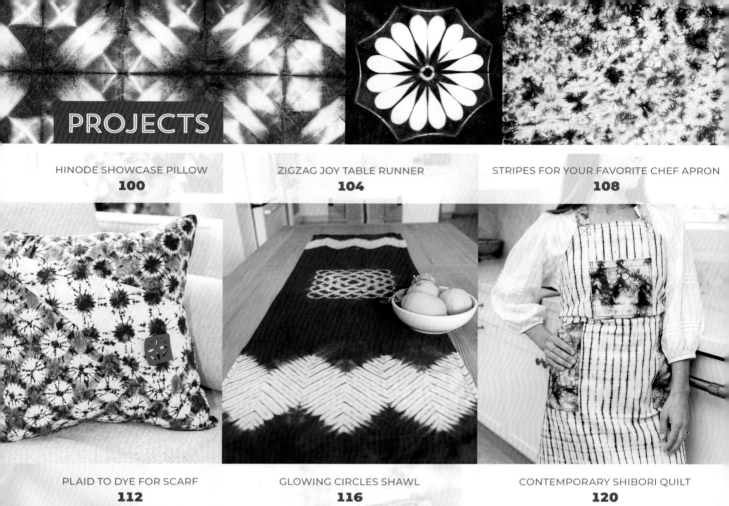

PROJECTS

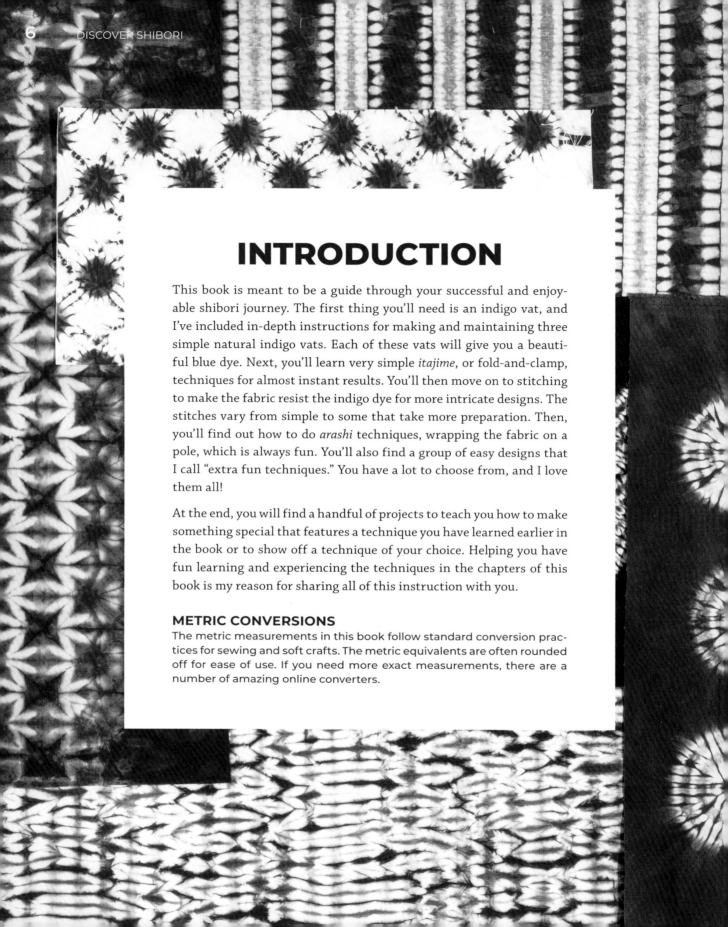

INTRODUCTION

This book is meant to be a guide through your successful and enjoyable shibori journey. The first thing you'll need is an indigo vat, and I've included in-depth instructions for making and maintaining three simple natural indigo vats. Each of these vats will give you a beautiful blue dye. Next, you'll learn very simple *itajime*, or fold-and-clamp, techniques for almost instant results. You'll then move on to stitching to make the fabric resist the indigo dye for more intricate designs. The stitches vary from simple to some that take more preparation. Then, you'll find out how to do *arashi* techniques, wrapping the fabric on a pole, which is always fun. You'll also find a group of easy designs that I call "extra fun techniques." You have a lot to choose from, and I love them all!

At the end, you will find a handful of projects to teach you how to make something special that features a technique you have learned earlier in the book or to show off a technique of your choice. Helping you have fun learning and experiencing the techniques in the chapters of this book is my reason for sharing all of this instruction with you.

METRIC CONVERSIONS

The metric measurements in this book follow standard conversion practices for sewing and soft crafts. The metric equivalents are often rounded off for ease of use. If you need more exact measurements, there are a number of amazing online converters.

THE BASICS OF
SHIBORI

Shibori is the ancient art of making fabric resist dye by stitching, folding, clamping, and/or pole wrapping it to make designs. You can select one technique or combine several techniques in one piece. The word *shibori* comes from the Japanese word *shiboru*, which means "to wring or squeeze."

In this technique, fabrics are manipulated in a variety of ways so that portions are compressed and will resist dye. These fabrics are then dyed, but the dye cannot reach the compressed portions, resulting in a variety of patterns once the fabric is released. The technique is believed to have come to Japan from China more than a millennium ago. It is sometimes mistakenly referred to as tie-dye, but shibori is far more complex. Many traditional designs are created with these methods of resisting dye, and there are always new ways to achieve beautiful results.

WHERE IT ALL STARTED

Photo by dowraik/Shutterstock.com

A BRIEF HISTORY OF SHIBORI

Resist dyeing was adapted in a specific way by the Japanese, and shibori dyeing is one of the oldest indigo dyeing techniques. Shibori was originally a process favored by the poor in ancient Japan because the average person could not afford to buy expensive fabrics, such as cotton or silk. The poor used less expensive hemp fabrics, which were repaired and redyed to extend their life. The art of shibori evolved to make old, faded, and worn clothes look new. Later, shibori also became a method of decorating silk kimonos for the rich as well as creating folk art for the poor. Shibori gained mainstream appeal during the cultural and artistic enlightenment of the Edo period (1603–1868). The love of shibori has endured—in fact, increasing in popularity over time—and shibori designs can be seen in apparel, home decorations, and fine art around the world.

People in many African countries use shibori techniques to decorate clothing and other textiles. The Yoruba people of southern Nigeria are well known for their decorative and highly intricate dyeing techniques, called Àdìrę.

Youruba Àdìrę cloth featuring the fishbone design

The people of Mali create designs such as guinea fowl, which resembles the patterns on feathers from the bird of the same name, and arrowhead, which resembles the tips of arrows. These, along with many others, are culture-specific or most commonly made by the Malians.

Malian dye patterns, cowry shell (left) and whip stitch (right)

Three major resist techniques are used in shibori: Itajime shibori uses folding, clamping, or wrapping to achieve designs; stitched shibori uses hand or machine stitching to resist dye; and arashi shibori involves wrapping fabrics around poles and binding them with string or thread. Each of these styles has numerous variations that yield boundless results. The dye most commonly used for traditional shibori is indigo.

A BRIEF HISTORY OF INDIGO

When you say *indigo*, you can be talking about a color, a plant, or a dye. Beautiful indigo blue is found in the leaves of specific plants around the world. Most of us know it as the color of blue jeans, but the oldest known fabric dyed with indigo dates back 6,000 years and was discovered in Huaca Prieta, Peru. Many countries and areas of the world, such as India, China, Japan, Africa, South America, and Southeast Asia, have used indigo as a dye for centuries.

Historians believe that people in India were the first to domesticate a plant now identified as *Indigofera tinctoria*. The deep blue dye they extracted was exported to the East and to the West. *Indigo* means "the Indian" or "from India," but species of indigo plants are found around the world. Indigo is the only natural blue dye.

Indigo became such an important cash crop that it caused trade wars and was a major contributing factor to slavery in the American colonies. Natural indigo fell from favor as a dye after the first production of a less expensive synthetic dye in the late 1800s. Synthetic indigo is manufactured from raw materials obtained from the petrochemical industry and can be very harmful to the environment and to the people making and using it. The resurgence of interest in the beautiful blue hue and the art of shibori has rekindled demand for the natural product. Many people are going back to the roots of indigo blue and again using the ecologically safer natural dye.

TOP *Indigofera tinctoria* from India
Photo by Pangni/Shutterstock.com

BOTTOM *Indigo persecaria tinctoria* from Japan

SETTING AND MAINTAINING AN INDIGO VAT

The techniques in this book use only all-natural indigo that is extracted from plants, dried, and ground to make a powder. The extraction methods are different in some countries.

In India, a water extraction method is used to make a paste that is dried and ground into a powder. In Japan, the dried indigo leaves are usually composted, dried, and fermented to make a special dye vat called *sukomo*. I'll explain how to make an organic indigo reduction vat that uses natural indigo powder from India.

Preparing indigo for dyeing is called *setting the vat*. A vat container can be a plastic bucket, a stainless-steel pan, or a ceramic vessel specially made for indigo dyeing. Indigo powder is insoluble in plain water. Creating the dye vat requires three ingredients in addition to water to make the indigo usable:

• Indigo powder for the dye

• Something to raise the pH of the water

• A reducing agent to remove oxygen from the water

The pH of the vat needs to be between 10 and 12. The correct pH is determined by the fibers being dyed. Protein fibers are happy with a pH of around 10, whereas the pH of a vat when dyeing cellulose can be as high as 12.

The third ingredient, which removes the oxygen from the vat, creates what is called a *reduction*. All the ingredients work together to form an environment that allows the indigo to attach to the fibers and dye the fabric. If all of these elements are not included, the indigo will not attach to the fabric, and it will remain undyed. If the amount of each ingredient is wrong, the indigo will not properly dissolve and won't dye the fabric or fibers.

Photo by Abel Tumik/Shutterstock.com

THREE NATURAL INDIGO VATS

This section includes instructions for making three different natural indigo vats.

Two of the vat recipes follow the guidelines introduced by Michel Garcia, a French botanist and chemist, for an all-natural vat that uses no harsh chemicals. It is called the *1, 2, 3 vat* because the ingredients are measured as one part, two parts, or three parts, depending on the type of vat. The third vat follows guidelines from Maiwa Textiles in Canada. Even though none of the ingredients are harsh, they should be stored safely and kept away from children and pets. You should always wear a KN95 respirator mask when working with dry powders. This type is not a full respirator but a respiratory protective mask designed to achieve a close facial fit and efficient filtration of airborne particles. Do not breathe in the airborne particles from any of the powders used in setting an indigo vat. The powders are not toxic—they just don't belong in your lungs. It is so much better and easier to be safe in the beginning rather than sorry later.

MEASURING INDIGO

The instructions for creating each of the vats give the amount of indigo and other powders needed in metric measurements. These powders need to be measured precisely, and typical imperial dry measurements are not exact enough. However, because the amount of liquid required is less specific, metric *and* imperial measurements are provided for liquids in the vat recipes.

GENERAL SUPPLIES FOR SETTING A VAT

When setting an indigo vat, you need to have some supplies on hand regardless of the type of vat you've chosen. The general supplies below are used for setting all types of indigo vats.

KITCHEN SAFETY
You need dedicated dye supplies. *Never* use your kitchen items for dyeing. Once they have been used for dyeing, your implements should never be used to prepare, store, or serve food.

When setting, maintaining, and using a vat, have the following items handy:

1. Kitchen scale to measure ingredients.

2. Medium plastic jar with marbles and a tight-fitting lid to hydrate the indigo.

3. Small and large metal spoons.

4. Containers for measuring powders. These can be bowls or recycled plastic containers, such as washed yogurt or cottage-cheese containers.

5. Two 5-gallon (19L) plastic buckets, including one with a lid, **or** a 5-gallon pot with a lid that can go on top of a heat source plus a plastic bucket for wetting fabrics. If you plan to use a bucket heater or immersion heater to warm the fructose or banana vats, a plastic bucket is fine, but if you plan to heat the vats with a direct source of heat, such as a burner, you will need to use a heat-safe pot.

6. Immersion heater to safely heat the liquid **if** you will be making a vat in a plastic bucket. These are commonly used for preventing ice in livestock water containers. You can use other types of heaters to keep the vat warm, such as aquarium heaters or electric blanket–style heaters.

7. Two 2- or 3-gallon (8–11L) buckets or tubs to be used as drip and rinse buckets. The rinse bucket needs to be large enough to allow you to immerse your entire project.

8. Long dowel for stirring the vat.

9. KN95 respirator face mask with a close facial fit to wear when measuring powders.

10. Tarp and/or plastic drop cloths to protect surfaces.

11. Newspapers or old towels to catch drips. I use old towels to catch drips and clean the area, and I keep a towel on my lap when dyeing to wipe drips from my gloves during the dyeing process.

12. Long dishwashing gloves to wear when dipping fabrics in dye.

13. Disposable gloves to wear when measuring ingredients and removing resists.

14. Instant-read thermometer to check the temperature of the vat.

15. Strainer for catching marbles when adding hydrated indigo to the vat.

16. pH strips to check the pH of the vat. I prefer to use plastic strips with four small test squares instead of paper strips because it is easier to read the area corresponding to the pH numbers on the box. See Taking the pH of the Vat (page 16) for a photo of my favorite test strips.

*Not pictured but also handy are small strips of scoured fabric about 1″ (2.5cm) wide and 12″ (30.5cm) long to test the vat (see Scouring, page 28).

Taking the pH of the Vat

The pH of the indigo vat is very important. For indigo to attach to fibers, it must be in an environment that will allow the indigo to change to a soluble material in the water. The vat must have a pH of at least 10 to 11. This is called a reduced vat.

It is difficult to take the pH of an indigo vat because if you dip the entire test strip into the vat, it will be covered in blue indigo. I use plastic pH test strips with four indicator squares.

1. Bend the strip to form an L shape, with the squares on the side of the L.

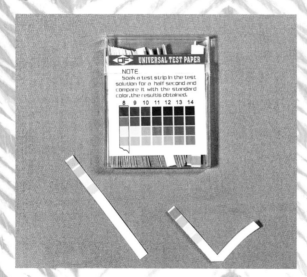

2. Push the flower and metallic sheen to the side.

3. Quickly touch, or kiss, the long L side of the strip to the top of the dye. Do not immerse it. The part of the strip that enters the indigo will be blue, but the liquid will wick up to the squares in one area.

4. Compare the area of the pH strip where the liquid wicked to the squares on the pH strip box to determine the pH of the dye.

PREPARING THE INDIGO

The simplest way to hydrate indigo powder requires only a few basic tools. Powdered indigo is just that—a dry powder made from extracted indigo pigment. The powder needs to be partially hydrated or wet before being added to the vat. The easiest way is to measure indigo powder into a jar with marbles, add **cold** water, cover the jar tightly, and shake it for 3 or 4 minutes. If you have any doubt about the lid of the jar being water-tight, place a towel over the lid before shaking the jar. Shaking partially hydrates the indigo powder, making it easier to dissolve. Add the hydrated indigo to the bucket, catching the marbles in a strainer.

Advanced Indigo Preparation

In the best vats I have set, I hydrated the indigo powder by using a mortar and pestle. The tool is an added expense but gives beautiful results. Place the indigo powder in a medium to large mortar. Add 1 tablespoon (15mL) of water at a time as you grind the indigo. Continue grinding and adding very small amounts of water until you have a loose paste. Keep grinding until the paste is shiny and almost appears to have stars sparkling on the surface (this process can take 20–30 minutes). Once the paste is hydrated, pour it into the vat and then rinse the mortar and pestle with reserved water.

STIRRING A VAT

After following the steps to create each type of vat, you need to maintain that vat's environment as much as possible (oxygen-free environment with a pH of at least 10–12). Stirring liquids can introduce oxygen, so how you mix the vat will make a difference in how your dye reacts. Using a dowel, stir the vat in a circular motion around the sides of the container, being careful to not create oxygen bubbles. Do not agitate the liquid—just move the dowel around the outside. A vortex or little funnel will form in the middle of the vat, bringing ingredients up from the bottom to mix everything together. Stir for about 3 minutes.

To stop the mixing action, place the dowel against the side of the vessel.

After you have finished stirring, cover the vat and allow it to set for 30 minutes to one hour to allow everything to settle again.

FRUCTOSE VAT

This type is one of the easiest indigo vats to set and yields a beautiful clear blue color. Darker blue shades require multiple dips.

The ingredient that removes oxygen from the water is fructose. Note: It *must* be fructose, not sucrose or table sugar. The fructose vat also requires reheating to dye properly. Remember, a fructose vat likes to be warm.

The following ingredients are needed to set a 4½ gallon (17L) medium-dark fructose vat:

1 part natural indigo = 100 grams

2 parts lime or calcium hydroxide to raise the pH = 200 grams

3 parts natural fructose to remove oxygen from the vat = 300 grams

Setting the Fructose Vat

1. Use a scale and small containers to measure out all the ingredients.

2. Heat 4½ gallons (17L) of water to about 180°F (82°C).

3. Add 4 gallons (15L) of the heated water to a 5-gallon (19L) bucket. Reserve ½ gallon (2L) of hot water to mix ingredients and rinse the utensils.

4. Dissolve the lime in some of the reserved hot water and add it to the 5-gallon (19L) bucket. Rinse the container with more of the reserved water and add it to the bucket.

5. Dissolve the fructose in some of the reserved hot water and add it to the bucket. Rinse the container with more of the reserved water and add it to the bucket.

6. Add the indigo to the jar with the marbles, pour in **cold** water, cover the jar tightly, and shake it for 3 or 4 minutes. This agitation will partially hydrate the indigo powder, making it easier to

dissolve. Add the hydrated indigo to the bucket, catching the marbles in a strainer.

7. Rinse the marbles and container with some of the reserved hot water and add it to the bucket.

8. Stir the vat with the dowel in a circular motion along the edge of the bucket, being careful to not create bubbles.

9. After stirring for about 3 minutes, let the vat settle for about 30 minutes. Repeat, stirring and resting twice. You will see a beautiful dark blue group of bubbles with undissolved indigo particles in the center of the vat surface; this group is called the *flower*. The surface of the vat will start to have a metallic sheen.

10. Push the flower to the side and dip a spoonful of liquid from the top of the vat with a large spoon. The liquid should be a translucent gold or amber, not blue. If the liquid is blue, stir the vat again and let it rest. Check to be sure that you added all the ingredients and that the water was hot to begin with. If anything was left out, add it now. If the water was cold or is no longer warm, heat it to 180°F (82°C).

11. Slowly swirl the dye in the spoon and watch as it starts to turn blue.

12. Wet a small test strip of fabric and place it in the vat. After about 5 minutes, remove the strip. It should appear green before starting to turn blue.

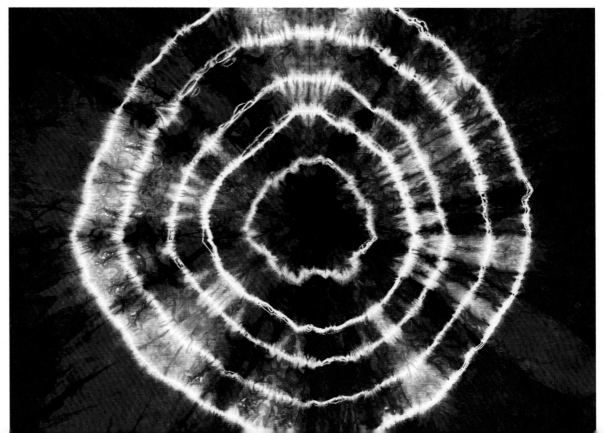

13. Remove the flower and set it aside in the drip container while dyeing. At the end of the dyeing session, pour the liquid from the drip container back into the vat, stir, and cover the vat with the lid.

Technically, your vat is ready to use, but a fructose vat will improve and become more beautiful after a couple of days. Fructose vats work best when warm. Be prepared to heat a fructose vat before each dyeing session by using a bucket heater or by placing the vat in a larger container with very hot water. When using the fructose vat on subsequent days, heat it to between 90°F (32°C) and 120°F (49°C).

To maintain a fructose vat, occasionally take the pH to see whether you need to add more lime; the minimum pH of your vat should be 9. If your pH is low, add approximately 14 grams of lime at a time. If a vat is hungry for lime, it will grab it immediately. Keep adding 14 grams at a time until the lime sits on the surface of the vat. Stir the vat and let it rest for about an hour before testing the pH again.

As you work with the vat, test it occasionally with a small strip of fabric to see whether it is still dyeing the material green before turning blue. If the strip is coming out blue instead of green, it either needs to be stirred and rested to allow the dye to reduce again after the action of repeated dipping or it may need more fructose. After stirring and resting the vat for at least one hour, test it again with a strip of fabric. If the fabric is still coming out blue, add about 50 grams of fructose dissolved in warm water. Stir and rest for at least an hour before testing again.

You will need to feed the vat 50 grams of fructose after a lot of dyeing to keep the reduction going.

I usually feed a fructose vat at the end of the day, stir, and let it rest overnight. If the pH drops below 6 your vat could develop mold. If you are not going to dye frequently you can avoid mold by checking the pH of your vat every 2 to 3 weeks and adjust as necessary to keep your pH at about 10.

IRON VAT

An iron vat, sometimes called a ferrous vat, will give you a cool blue with a slightly gray cast. It is a good choice for darker blue shades, but do note that darker shades still require multiple dips.

An iron vat is easy to maintain, and you can use it at room temperature without reheating the contents. The large amounts of lime in this vat can damage protein fibers, so it is not recommended for use on silk or wool. As you work with the vat, test it occasionally with a small strip of fabric to see whether it is still dyeing the material green and then turning blue. If the strip is coming out blue instead of green, the vat needs to be stirred and rested to allow the dye to reduce again.

IMPORTANT SAFETY NOTE
Iron (ferrous sulfate) in high doses is unsafe for babies, small children, and pets. It is not known whether iron residue remains on the fabric and in the vat in amounts that could be of concern. **Out of an abundance of caution, we recommend use of this vat by adults only.** Store iron in a secure location and away from children and pets.

The following ingredients are needed to set a 4½ gallon (17L) medium-dark iron vat:

  1 part natural indigo = 80 grams

  2 parts ferrous sulfate (iron) = 160 grams

  3 parts lime or calcium hydroxide = 240 grams

Setting the Iron Vat

1. Use a scale and small containers to measure out all the ingredients.

2. Heat 4½ gallons (17L) of water to about 180°F (82°C).

3. Add 4 gallons (15L) of the heated water to the 5-gallon (19L) bucket. Reserve ½ gallon (2L) of hot water to mix ingredients and rinse the utensils.

4. Dissolve the lime in some of the reserved hot water and add it to the 5-gallon (19L) bucket. Rinse the container with more of the reserved hot water and add it to the bucket.

5. Dissolve the ferrous sulfate in some of the reserved hot water and add it to the bucket. Rinse the container with more of the reserved water and add it to the bucket.

6. Add indigo to the jar with the marbles, pour in **cold** water, cover the jar tightly, and shake it for 3 or 4 minutes. This process will partially hydrate the indigo powder, making it easier to dissolve. Add the hydrated indigo to the bucket, catching the marbles in a strainer.

7. Rinse the marbles and container with more of the reserved hot water and add it to the bucket.

8. Stir the vat with the dowel in a circular motion along the edge of the bucket, being careful to not create bubbles.

9. After stirring for about 3 minutes, let the vat settle for about 30 minutes. Repeat stirring and resting twice. You will see a beautiful dark blue group of bubbles with undissolved indigo particles in the center of the vat surface. This group is called the *flower*. The surface of the vat will have a metallic sheen.

10. Push the flower to the side and dip a spoonful of liquid from the top of the vat with a large spoon. The liquid should be a translucent gold or amber, not blue. If the liquid is still blue, stir again and let it rest for 30 minutes. Check to be sure that you added all the ingredients and that the water was hot to begin with. If anything was left out, add it now. If the water was cold or is no longer warm, heat it now to 180°F (82°C).

11. Slowly swirl the dye in the spoon and watch as it starts to turn blue.

12. Wet one of the small strips of fabric and place it in the vat. After about 5 minutes, remove the strip of fabric. It should be green and start to turn blue.

Your vat is ready to use as soon as it is cool enough to put gloved hands into and does not require reheating. Remove the flower and set it aside before dyeing.

13. At the end of the dyeing session, put the flower and the liquid from the drip container back into the vat.

14. Stir and let the dye settle, and cover the vat with a lid. This lid is all that is needed to maintain an iron vat. Additional heat or ingredients are not required.

BANANA VAT

A banana vat is reliable, gives a clear bright blue, and smells great. It requires multiple dips for darker shades and likes to be heated. All natural fibers can be dyed in a fruit vat, and it can be used by all ages. Other fruits that are high in sugar, such as dates or pears, can also be used to make a fruit vat.

The following ingredients are needed to set a 4½ gallon (17L) banana reduced vat:

  75 grams natural indigo

  40 grams lime or calcium hydroxide (may need more later to raise the pH)

  7 pounds (3kg) very ripe bananas

Setting the Banana Vat

1. Peel the bananas and discard the peels. Mash the bananas and add them to a large pot with approximately 1 gallon (4L) of water. Bring to a boil and then simmer for about 30 minutes. Take care to keep it from burning or boiling over by stirring often.

2. Use a scale and small containers to measure out the indigo and lime.

3. Heat 3½ gallons (13L) of water to about 120°F (49°C).

4. Add 3 gallons (11L) to the 5-gallon (19L) bucket. Reserve ½ gallon (2L) of the hot water to mix ingredients and rinse the utensils.

5. Strain the banana liquid into the vat, saving the pulp in a zippered plastic bag in the refrigerator for up to 3 days. If you need to feed the vat within that time, you can boil the reserved pulp again. You can do this approximately three times before needing new bananas. Each time you reboil the pulp, do so in approximately ½ gallon (2L) of water and use the resulting liquid (with pulp strained out) to maintain the vat. You can also boil the pulp ahead of time, strain it, and then save the resulting liquid in the refrigerator for up to 3 days or in the freezer for up to 3 months.

6. Dissolve the lime in some of the reserved hot water and add it to the bucket. Rinse the container with more of the reserved water and add it to the bucket.

7. Add indigo to the jar with the marbles, pour in **cold** water, cover the jar tightly, and shake it for 3 or 4 minutes. This process will partially hydrate the indigo powder, making it easier to dissolve. Add the hydrated indigo to the bucket, catching the marbles in a strainer.

8. Rinse the marbles and container with some of the reserved hot water and add it to the bucket.

9. Stir the vat with the dowel in a circular motion along the edge of the bucket, being careful to not create bubbles.

10. After stirring for about 3 minutes, let the vat settle for about 30 minutes. Repeat stirring and resting two or three times and then cover the vat with the lid. Allow the banana vat to rest overnight.

11. Before heating the vat for use, test its pH. It should be at least 10 to 12. If the pH is not at least 10, check to be sure that you added all the ingredients and that the water was hot to begin with. If anything was left out, add it now. If the vat is cold, heat it to 120°F (49°C).

12. Stir the vat. You will see a beautiful dark blue group of bubbles with undissolved indigo particles in the center of the vat surface. This group is called the *flower*. The surface of the vat will have a metallic sheen.

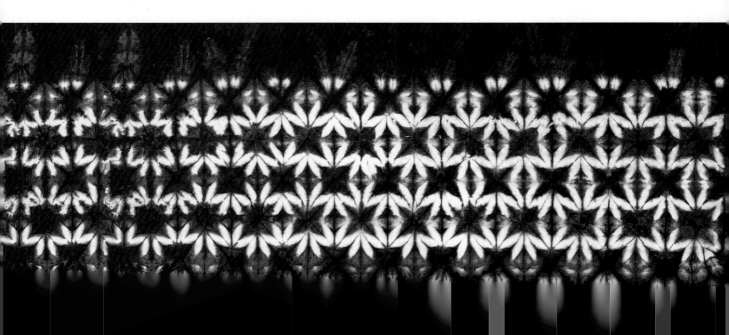

13. Push the flower to the side and dip a spoonful of liquid from the top of the vat with a large spoon. The liquid should be a translucent gold or amber, not blue. If the liquid is blue, check to be sure that you added all the ingredients. If you added everything initially, heat the vat, stir it, and wait until the next day. Sometimes, a fruit vat may take a little longer to be ready to use. Be patient.

14. Slowly swirl the dye in the spoon and watch as it starts to turn blue.

15. Wet one of the small strips of fabric and place it in the vat. After about 5 minutes, remove the strip of fabric. It should be yellow-green and then start to turn blue. If your strip isn't yellow-green or does not begin to turn blue, check the pH and the temperature of the vat again and adjust as necessary. If both the pH and temperature are okay, stir the vat and let it rest overnight and try another test strip.

Your vat is ready to use. Remove the flower and set it aside before dyeing. At the end of the dyeing session, put the flower and the liquid from the drip container back into the vat, stir, and cover it with the lid.

This vat will improve and become more beautiful after a couple of days. Fruit vats work best when warm. Be prepared to heat a banana vat before each use by using a bucket heater or by placing the vat inside a larger container of very hot water. When using the banana vat on subsequent days, heat it to about 90°F (32°C) to 120°F (49°C). To maintain the banana vat after a lot of dyeing, add more liquid from the boiled banana pulp, about 1 cup (240mL) at a time. If you no longer have liquid from boiling bananas, maintain the vat by adding ¼ cup (60mL) of fructose. Test the pH. If it is below 10, add lime, about 14 grams at a time. If a vat is hungry for lime, it will grab it immediately. Keep adding 14 grams at a time until the lime sits on the surface of the vat. Stir the vat and let it rest for about an hour before testing the pH again.

CHOOSING SUITABLE FABRICS AND PREPARING THEM FOR INDIGO DYE

Indigo will dye only all-natural fibers. Natural fibers are made from plants or animals. Synthetic fibers, such as polyester, will not take indigo dye.

CELLULOSE FIBERS

Cellulose fibers come from plant sources, including cotton, linen, hemp, ramie, and bamboo.

PROTEIN FIBERS

Protein fibers are derived from animals, such as sheep, goats, rabbits, and even silkworms. Examples are wool, cashmere, mohair, alpaca, angora, and silk. Feathers are also made of protein and can be dyed. For shibori dyeing, you will most likely be using silk or a very finely woven wool.

COMBINATION FIBERS

Combination fabrics combine two or more fibers in one fabric. They can be combinations of cellulose, protein, or a mix of both sources of fiber. It is important to know whether your fabric contains protein fibers so that you can select the correct method of scouring.

Dried flax plant on pure linen fabric
Photo by BartTa/Shutterstock.com

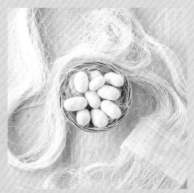

Silkworm cocoons and fibers
Photo by Berna Namoglu/Shutterstock.com

This combination of silk and cotton will need to be scoured as if it were all silk.

SCOURING

All fibers must be clean and free of starches, sizing, or oils so they will dye properly and retain the color. This process is called scouring. Scouring removes anything that may be on the fabrics that could act as a resist and prevent the indigo from attaching to the fabric.

Scouring is extremely important when working with vintage fabrics that could have dust or dirt from storage or any fabric that has not been labeled as prepared for dyeing, which could have starch or sizing added. Even fabrics labeled as prepared for dyeing need to be lightly scoured to remove oils from being handled or small amounts of starch that may have been added to make the fabrics look pretty when they are pressed and put on bolts.

There are two basic scouring methods, one for cellulose fibers and one for protein fibers. When scouring a combination fabric that contains a protein fiber, **always** scour by using the method for protein fibers.

You will need to have some supplies on hand for all types of scouring:

1. A pot large enough to allow the fabrics to move freely when submerged.

2. Neutral detergent for the type of fabric being scoured. Protein and cellulose fibers are scoured with different methods. Refer to the following instructions to determine the correct detergent for the specific fibers being scoured.

3. A kitchen scale and small container to weigh dry fabric.

4. Heat source.

Before scouring, weigh the dry fibers to determine the amount of detergent to use:

1. Set the scale to pounds and ounces.

2. Place a container large enough to hold the fabric on the scale.

3. Push the tare button to bring the reading to zero. The tare button will be labeled on the scale.

4. Place your fabrics in the container that is already on the scale.

5. Record the weight.

Scouring Cellulose Fibers

To scour cellulose fibers, you will need detergent and soda ash. Use a neutral detergent, such as Original Dawn dishwashing detergent or Synthrapol (a concentrated wetting agent) at 2 teaspoons (10mL) per pound of fabric. Soda ash (sodium carbonate) is used to lower the pH of the bath and aid in cleaning. You will need 1½ tablespoons (22mL) of soda ash per pound of fabric.

To be sure that you have enough room for the fabric to move around freely in the pot, add the dry fabric to the empty pot to see how full it is. The fabric will compress when wet, but you will get a good idea of whether there is enough room. If the pot is too crowded, find a larger pot or scour your fabric in batches. Remove your fabric from the pot and follow the process outlined below:

1. Fill your pot with enough water to cover the fabric and allow it room to spread out a bit so you can be sure to reach all areas.

2. Add the liquid detergent.

3. Dissolve the soda ash in water and add it to the pot.

4. Add the fabric and bring the pot to a boil. Stirring occasionally, let it simmer for 1 hour. Add more water if necessary.

5. The water in the pot will become cloudy and take on a brownish color. If the water in the pot is very brown, you may want to discard it and repeat the process. Allow the water to cool slightly, remove the fabric from the pot, and rinse it thoroughly.

Scouring Protein Fibers

To scour protein fibers, you will need a detergent that is safe for wool or protein fibers, such as Orvus WA Paste, Eucalan, or another neutral detergent at 1 teaspoon (5mL) per pound of fiber.

To be sure you have enough room for the fabric to move around freely in the pot, add the dry fabric to the empty pot to see how full it is. It will compress when wet, but you will get a good idea of whether there is enough room. If the pot is too crowded, find a larger pot or scour your fabric in batches. Remove your fabric from the pot and follow the process outlined below:

1. Fill your pot with enough **slightly warm** water to cover the fabric and allow it room to spread out a bit so you can be sure to reach all areas.

2. Add the liquid detergent.

3. Carefully add the fabric and **slowly** bring the temperature to 140°F (60°C). Maintain the temperature for 1 hour, occasionally stirring gently.

4. Allow the fabric to cool in the pot. Remove it from the pot and rinse it thoroughly, but gently, in warm water.

TREAT WOOL GENTLY
To prevent wool or wool blends from felting, never move them directly from a hot water bath to cold water or be too vigorous when stirring. **Always be gentle.**

HOW TO DYE IN THE VAT

Your vat is made and tested and your fabrics are scoured and rinsed. You are now ready to dye in the indigo! Skip ahead to Major Techniques of Shibori (page 33) to select your design and prepare your fabric for dyeing. Follow the steps below to dye your bundled fabric items.

DIPPING

1. Remove the flower and place it in a small container.

2. Most items to be dyed must be *wetted out* (the process of placing the shibori resisted fabric in a bucket of water to soak) before being dipped in the indigo vat. This process keeps the prepared shibori bundles from releasing oxygen into the vat and helps prevent *wicking*, or drawing of the indigo dye under the resists where the dry fibers are. If the fibers in the bundle are tightly resisted and fully wet, they will not wick indigo. To wet out your item, fill an extra bucket with warm water. Place your prepared item in the water for a few minutes until it is completely wet and you do not see any bubbles rising. Remove your item and squeeze it to remove any excess water.

3. With your gloves on, slip the item into the indigo vat and keep it submerged for about 10 minutes. Do not move the bundle in and out; just leave it in the dye until the time is up.

4. While your item is still immersed in the vat, squeeze it to remove excess dye and then immediately remove it from the vat and hold it over a drip bucket so that any remaining dye does not drip back into the vat and introduce oxygen. When the fabric is removed from the indigo vat, it will be green or yellow-green.

5. Hang the item to allow the indigo to oxidize; all the green will turn blue. This process can take 5 to 30 minutes, depending on the weight of the fabric and how detailed the resists are. The entire surface must be oxidized, or blue, on the outside surfaces before being dipped again. Do not remove any resists, but do open pleats or folds to check that all green is now blue.

6. If you are using an iron vat, lightly rinse your item in plain water after each dip to remove excess lime and any particles that may cling to the item. If you are using a fructose or banana vat, rinse your item lightly after every three or four dips.

7. Achieve darker shades of indigo through multiple rounds of dipping and oxidizing. Dip your items as many times as necessary to achieve the depth of color you desire. Remember, the fabric will be at least two or three shades lighter when dry.

At the end of the session, put the liquid from the drip bucket and the saved flower back into the vat and stir.

ACHIEVING DARK BLUES
Darker blues are achieved by multiple dips. You may need as many as ten to get a very dark, intense indigo blue.

OPENING THE BUNDLES
Allow your dyed items to set overnight to finish oxidizing. Then, do the following:

1. Add 1 drop of neutral detergent to a bucket of water to wash and then rinse the bundle very vigorously **before** removing the resists.

2. Carefully remove the resists and rinse the fabric again in cool water.

3. To neutralize the lime from the dye, place the fabric in a *vinegar rinse*. In a bucket, add ¼ cup (60mL) plain white vinegar per gallon (3.8L) of cold water. Add the dyed items and allow them to soak in the vinegar solution for about 10 to 30 minutes. This process will also brighten the color of the indigo.

4. Rinse the fabric lightly by swirling it in cold water and then hang it to dry.

5. Wait about two weeks before finishing.

CARING FOR THE VAT

An **iron vat** needs nothing added to keep using it. At the end of each dyeing session, pour the contents of the drip bucket and the flower back into the vat, stir it, cover the container, and let it settle.

A **fructose or banana vat** needs to be fed and the pH needs to be monitored:

1. Take the pH of the vat. If it is below 10, add about 14 grams of lime at a time. If the vat is hungry, it will absorb the lime almost instantaneously; you'll see this happen when you sprinkle it in. Keep adding lime 14 grams at a time until it sits on the surface of the vat. Stir the vat and let it rest for about an hour before testing the pH again.

2. If you have dyed a lot of fiber, you should add about ¼ cup (60mL) fructose or 1 cup (240mL) of boiled banana liquid to help reduce the vat.

3. Stir the vat and place the lid on the bucket.

4. When you're ready to use again, if the vat is cold, heat to around 90°F (32°C).

5. Always stir the vat, allow it to settle, and then test it with a strip of fabric. After 5 minutes, remove the test strip. It should be green and then begin to turn blue.

SIGNS OF AN EXHAUSTED VAT

All vats will eventually *exhaust*, or no longer dye. The first sign is that after the vat is stirred, the flower will be lighter blue and fabric test strips will come out light blue. If the vat is the correct temperature, the pH is at least 10 or 11, and you have fed the vat, but the fabric test strip is still not coming out green before turning blue, that may mean that the indigo in the vat has been used up. Always try stirring and allowing the vat to rest at least an hour or overnight. If you are still not getting a green test strip, your vat has probably used all the indigo. You can add more indigo, but if you are using a 5-gallon (19L) vat, it is usually easier to start over. A new vat gives you a fresh chance to be sure that you have all the ingredients in the correct amounts.

FINISHING THE FABRICS

Finishing is the process of applying heat to push the dye into the fabric fibers and remove any excess dye particles. After you have dyed your fabrics and put them in a vinegar bath to neutralize the lime, let them rest for two weeks before completing the final heated finish.

1. Place the dyed fabrics in a large pot of water.

2. Add a very small amount of neutral detergent, such as Original Dawn.

3. For cellulose fibers, bring the pot to a boil and boil for 10 minutes.

4. For protein fabrics or fibers, heat the pot slowly until you see steam but no bubbles and maintain this temperature for 10 minutes.

5. After allowing the fabrics to cool in the pot, remove them and give them a final wash in warm water with neutral detergent. Rinse in cold water until the water runs clear.

Dyed fabrics can be washed in cold water with neutral detergent. If you need to press indigo-dyed fabric, be sure to press from the wrong side.

MAJOR TECHNIQUES OF
SHIBORI

Shibori is a method of resist dyeing. In resist dyeing, fabrics are manipulated in such a way that portions are compressed and/or covered by stitches, shapes, or wrappings to avoid contact with the dye. The dye most commonly used for traditional shibori is indigo. These fabrics are then dyed, but the dye cannot reach the compressed portions, resulting in a variety of patterns once the fabric is released. Three major resist techniques are used in shibori: *Itajime* shibori uses folding and clamping, or wrapping, to achieve designs; *stitched* shibori uses hand stitching to resist the dye; and for *arashi* techniques, fabric is wrapped around poles and bound with string or thread. Each of these styles has numerous variations to achieve boundless designs.

For the most part, I share the techniques as I learned them. However, I do a few things just a bit differently than others might because I have found a few tricks that work well for me. When that is the case, I share my method with you.

ITAJIME SHIBORI

Itajime (Japanese for "board clamping") designs are achieved by first folding the fabric and then clamping identical shapes onto both sides of the folded fabric package before dyeing. Indigo dye can only dye what it can touch or "see," so the fabric is accordioned or fan-folded to allow the indigo dye to flow around the unclamped areas of the fabric. The shapes are clamped very tightly to resist the dye in certain places, creating designs. The results tend to feature bold patterns, such as repeated shapes separated by contrasting shades of blue.

Photo by C&T Publishing, Inc.

SUPPLIES

You will need a few supplies to get your fabric ready to dye:

1. Prepared fabric (scoured and pressed).

2. Shapes to use as resists. The shapes can be any shape and made of wood, acrylic, or metal.

3. Clamps to hold shapes in place.

4. Yarn, twine, or thread to wrap and tie around the folded fabric bundles in place of clamps.

5. Rubber bands to wrap around as a resist.

6. Clothespins, clips, or anything that will compress and hold fabric to resist the dye.

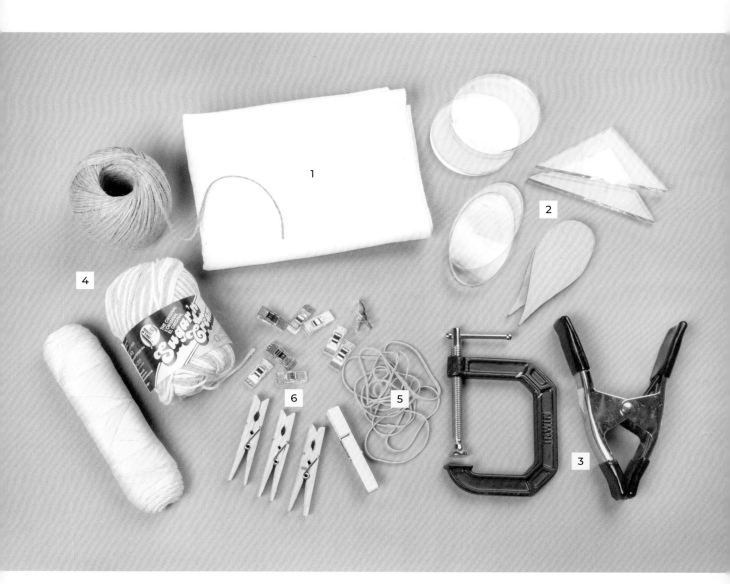

FIVE WAYS TO FOLD THE FABRIC

No matter which of the five fold shapes you want to achieve, folding for itajime usually starts with an accordion fold to allow the indigo to flow between the layers. If you want big bold designs, the initial fold can be a wide accordion fold. For tiny petite designs, you need smaller folds.

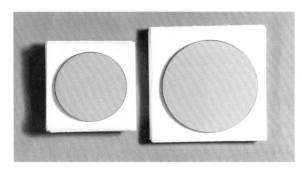

No matter the size of the design, the process is the same:

1. Fold the piece of fabric in half lengthwise.

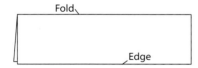

2. Bring the free edge of the top layer back to meet the fold, being sure to line up the fabric edge with the fold.

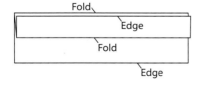

3. Turn the piece over and repeat Step 2.

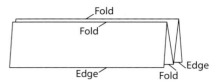

WHEN WORKING WITH LARGE PIECES OF FABRIC

If you are working with wider pieces of fabric, it may be easier to measure the width of the fabric, decide the width of the accordion folds, then measure the fabric as you create them.

For example, if your fabric is 60″ (152cm) wide and you want 4″ (10.2cm) folds, measure 4″ (10.2cm) down the width of the fabric and press the area back. You can then start folding back and forth at the 4″ (10.2cm) of the first fold. The last fold will only be 2″ (5.1cm) wide. Decide before placing any resists whether you want the final 2″ (5.1cm) to continue the resist pattern or whether you want to leave the final 2″ (5.1cm) hanging free to create a blue edge on the final design.

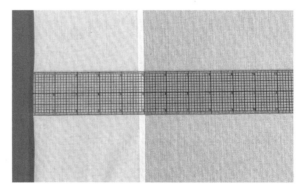

SQUARE FOLD

To make a square folded design, follow these steps:

1. Make the initial accordion fold. Lay the piece flat on a table.

2. Beginning on one end of the accordion-folded strip, keep one corner flat on the surface. Bring the other corner over to meet the opposite side of the long tail, making a triangle. Do not crease the triangle. Using your fingernail or a water-soluble marker, mark where the corner meets the fold.

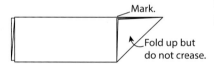

Mark.

Fold up but do not crease.

3. Lay the piece flat again and then fold it on the marked line to create a square. Flip the piece over and repeat.

Fold.

4. Keep folding back and forth to make an accordion-folded square.

When released, a square fold creates an even grid across the fabric.

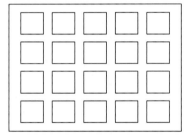

If you tie an identically shaped resist piece in the center of both sides of the folded square, you will get a grid of shapes resembling the resist shape, with faint echoes of the string or rubber bands.

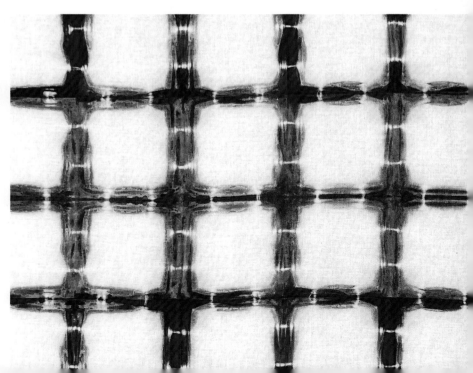

If you clamp an identically shaped resist piece in the center of both sides of the folded square, you will get a grid of shapes resembling the resist shape.

If you place the resist shapes off center, you will get groups of four shapes.

Placing resists on multiple corners will result in multiple groups of four shapes.

Beautiful designs can also be made by wrapping the folded square with string or rubber bands.

Once the piece is folded and your resists are in place, it is time to dye your fabric. Follow the instructions in How to Dye in the Vat (page 30) to dye, rinse, and finish your fabric

RIGHT-TRIANGLE FOLD

To make a right-triangle folded design, follow these steps:

1. Make the initial accordion fold. Lay the piece flat on a table.

2. Beginning on one end of the accordion-folded strip, keep one corner flat on the surface. Bring the other corner to meet the opposite side of the long tail and crease to make a right triangle.

3. Turn the piece over and fold the triangle accordion-style.

4. Crease and repeat the accordion folding back and forth, maintaining the right triangle.

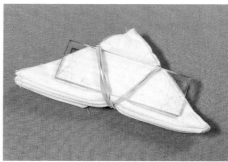

Placing resists on both sides in the center of the triangle will result in a circle of eight repeats of the resist shape.

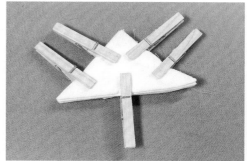

Placing resists along the edges of the triangle will make a fun repeated design.

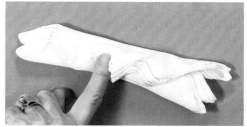

Smashing the center of the triangle and wrapping it with a string will create a diamond pattern.

Multiple resists will leave multiple circles of shapes.

Once the piece is folded and your resists are in place, it is time to dye your fabric. Follow the instructions in How to Dye in the Vat (page 30) to dye, rinse, and finish your fabric.

EQUILATERAL-TRIANGLE FOLD

To make an equilateral-triangle folded design, follow these steps:

1. Make the initial accordion fold. Lay the piece flat on a table.

2. Fold one end of your accordion-folded strip in half lengthwise to find the center of the strip. Gently crease to mark the center.

3. Beginning on one end of the accordion-folded strip, keep one corner flat on the surface. Fold the other corner to meet the center line and crease the small triangle.

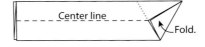

4. This triangle is what we are working with in this piece.

5. Turn the piece over. Fold the fabric back to form a full triangle.

6. Continue to fold back and forth, forming an accordion-folded equilateral triangle.

The final small amount of fabric (on the left) can be folded back or it can be left hanging. If it is left hanging there will be a dark blue edge to the piece.

Placing resists on both sides in the center of the triangle will result in a circle of six repeats of the resist shape.

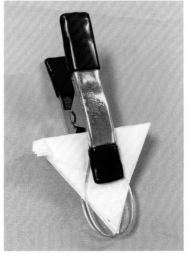

Placing resists on a corner of the triangle will result in small circles of six repeats each.

Using a larger resist across one corner will make a hexagon-shaped design.

Many different designs result from placing different resist shapes in different places.

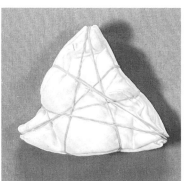

Place rubber bands crossing the points and centered on each side of the triangle.

Once the piece is folded and your resists are in place, it is time to dye your fabric. Follow the instructions in How to Dye in the Vat (page 30) to dye, rinse, and finish your fabric.

ASONOWA OR HEMP-LEAF FOLD

This is a particularly tricky fold. If following the text and illustrations still has you scratching your head, you can watch me demonstrate in a video.

To access the video through the tiny URL, type the web address below into your browser.

tinyurl.com/11561-video

To access the video through the QR code, open the camera app on your phone, aim the camera at the QR code, and click the link that pops up on the screen.

To make an *asonowa* (Japanese for "hemp leaf") design, follow these steps:

1. Make the initial accordion fold. Lay the piece flat on the table.

2. Fold one half of your accordion-folded strip in half lengthwise to find the center of the strip. Gently crease to mark the center. Lay the piece flat again.

3. Beginning on one end of the accordion-folded strip, keep one corner flat on the surface. Fold the other corner to meet the center line and crease the small triangle.

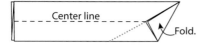

4. This triangle is what we are working with in this piece.

5. Turn the piece over and then fold the triangle back to the front so it meets the side of the long tail.

6. Turn the piece over and then bring the long tail back, meeting the side of the tail with the middle of the triangle at the point.

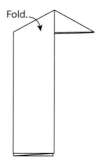

7. Bring it back up, making a fold on the bottom with the sides meeting on the center.

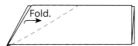

8. Fold the long tail over to meet the opposite short side of the triangle.

9. Fold the triangle back over and line up one short side along the long tail.

10. Repeat Steps 6–9 until finished.

The final small amount of fabric (on the left) can be folded back or it can be left hanging. If it is left hanging there will be a dark blue edge to the piece.

Place a rectangle resist across the folded fabric, allowing the points and edges to extend beyond the resist.

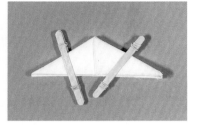

You can place bamboo sticks, chopsticks, or craft sticks across your folded bundle to create a variety of designs. I placed one stick vertically and one perpendicular to a long side to create the design to the top left.

Wrap string tightly around the side points and place a circle resist in the center This will make the design that is shown on the left bottom.

Once the piece is folded and your resists are in place, it is time to dye your fabric. Follow the instructions in How to Dye in the Vat (page 30) to dye, rinse, and finish your fabric.

MANDALA FOLD

This design does not start with a typical accordion fold; instead, it starts with a square or rectangle of fabric, laid flat on the table. The resists are added after a series of specific folds. To make a mandala folded design, follow these steps:

1. Fold the fabric in half, top to bottom. Fold the fabric again in half from side to side, crease lightly, and open this second fold.

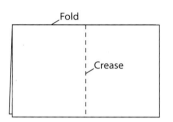

2. Bring the top left corner to meet the center crease. Repeat with the top right corner.

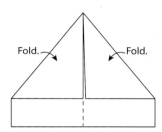

3. Bring the left corner back to meet the fold on the left side. Repeat with the right corner.

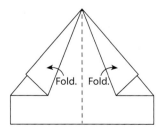

4. Turn the entire piece over. Bring the current left fold to the center. Bring the right fold to the center.

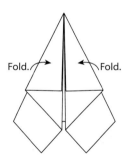

5. Turn the piece over. Bring the left side to meet the right side.

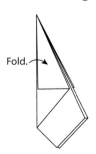

6. Place the resists on the folded fabric.

If you're using acrylic or wooden resists of any kind, you'll need identical resists on both sides. Any resist placed on the folded fabric will repeat 16 times around the final sample.

Once the piece is folded and your resists are in place, it is time to dye your fabric. Follow the instructions in How to Dye in the Vat (page 30) to dye, rinse, and finish your fabric.

KANOKO

This easy style is the one that most closely resembles classic Western tie-dye. *Kanoko* means "fawn" in Japanese, and the design can resemble the spots on a fawn.

Like their Western counterparts, kanoko artists often use elastic bands as well as threads to tie their fabric. It is said to be one of the easiest shibori techniques for beginners, allowing for personal creativity.

The piece can display one large design or multiple designs in different sizes. To try this type of resist, follow these steps:

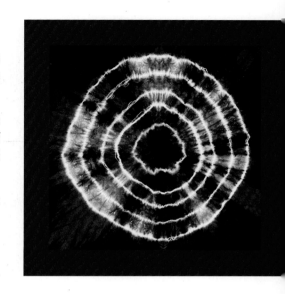

1. Pinch a portion of cloth, letting the fabric hang down.

2. Beginning at the top of the pinched fabric, tie a knot by using thread or place a rubber band around the fabric, close to the pinched portion.

3. Continue placing rubber bands or tying knots down the bundle of fabric.

4. Follow the instructions in How to Dye in the Vat (page 30) to dye, rinse, and finish your fabric.

TRY WRAPPING INSTEAD!
There is a second, and pretty fun, way to achieve this design. Skip ahead to Kumo (page 72) to find out how.

STITCH RESISTS

Stitches of many kinds are used to resist the indigo and make beautiful shibori designs.

This technique is almost like drawing with stitches. The stitches are usually simple, placed in a manner that gives stunning results. Most of the designs for stitched shibori are first marked and then stitched on the fabric. After the stitching is finished, the thread is pulled very tightly, gathering the fabric and compressing the stitches. The thread must be pulled as tightly as possible to compress the fabric so the indigo cannot reach the area. Compressing the fabric when the stitches are pulled is what creates the resist to make the designs.

Photo by C&T Publishing, Inc.

A secondary design develops when the stitches are pulled and compressed. The fabric in the area near the stitching is slightly compressed, which creates more shades of blue. If the fabric that is stitched is initially white, you can end up with white designs surrounded by shades of blue from very light to very dark, depending on how many times you dip the fabric.

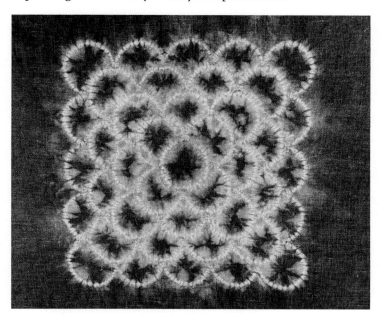

Making the same stitch but varying its length and how close the lines of stitching are to one another can create a variety of final results.

You can also stitch curved or wavy lines.

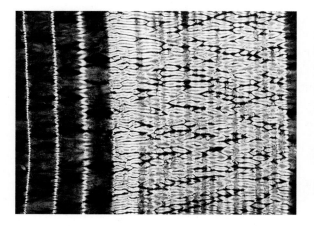

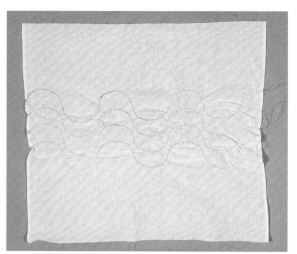

Shibori stitching can be very simple or very elaborate. Beyond just stitching straight or wavy lines, you can also stitch a motif onto your fabric before dyeing. Go for it! You might start easy and progress to more elaborate designs.

SUPPLIES

You will need a few supplies to get your fabric stitched and ready to dye.

1. **Needles:** Milliner and Sashiko needles are great for shibori stitching. A variety of different sizes is especially nice when you are learning.

2. **Thread for stitching:** Bonded nylon, such as heavy upholstery thread, is very strong and resists breaking. Use a lighter color that is not white so you can see your stitches, even after dyeing.

3. **Thread for wrapping:** For some techniques, I use 12-weight cotton thread, which is comparable to what is used in Japan.

4. **Thimble:** I wear a leather thimble on the middle finger of my dominant hand. You may prefer a metal thimble or a palm thimble.

5. Water-soluble marker—do not select air-erasable markers

6. See-through ruler

7. Small spray bottle

8. Small towel

9. Scissors

Optional: Adhesive bandage, medical tape, or a small piece of fabric to wrap around and protect your finger when pulling threads

Before you begin, select a design and decide how you will transfer it to your fabric. You can find a number of preprinted designs online, purchase a stencil, or draw your own design. You next need to transfer that design onto your fabric.

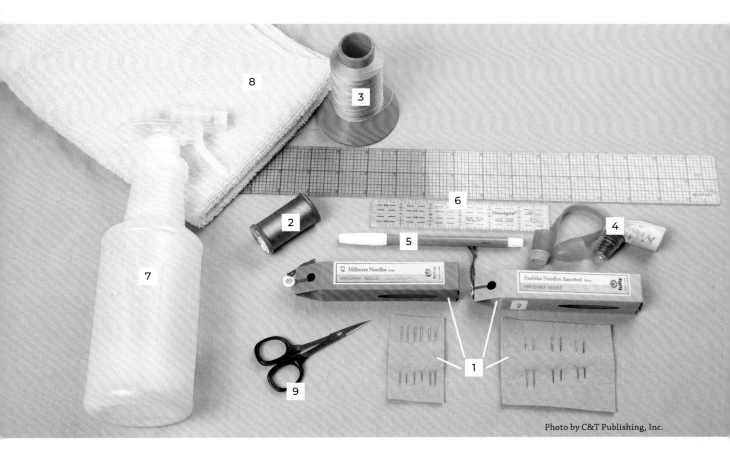

Photo by C&T Publishing, Inc.

SELECTING YOUR DESIGN

Before you mark your design onto your fabric, you first need to choose the design you want to make. Flip to Nui Shibori Designs (page 61) to select your design. Instructions with each of these designs indicate how to mark it.

If it is a repeated, geometric design, you may be able to simply use a ruler, a shibori stencil, or even a Sashiko stencil to mark dots onto your fabric. These dots will help you create even lines of stitches. Stencils specifically made for shibori stitching and pleating are fantastic tools to save time when marking stitch designs that you use frequently and to guarantee consistent results. I use stencils to mark dots for several different sizes of pleats for a variety of techniques.

For a more organic or curved design, such as a flower, you will probably want to trace the design onto the fabric so you can stitch around it. You can find simple designs to trace online, use the line drawings in coloring books, select a fun and pretty quilting stencil to use as a design, or draw your own design freehand!

Downloadable Designs

In case you want to try a more elaborate design before drafting your own, I've provided a couple for you. You can download the designs, select the one you want, and print it. Each diagram offers a design to trace, along with stitching instructions.

To access the downloadable designs through the tiny url, type the web address below into your browser.

tinyurl.com/11561-pattern1-download

To access the downloadable designs through the QR code, open the camera app on your phone, aim the camera at the QR code, and click the link that pops up on the screen.

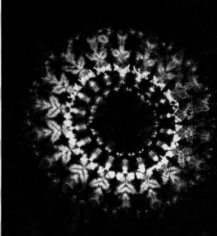

MARKING

Once you have selected your design, you are ready to begin marking. Press your fabric before marking. Remember to always use a water-soluble marker. Air-erasable options are not suitable because the design may disappear before you finish stitching. Permanent pens can leave unwanted marks on the fabric, and heat-erasable markers can potentially leave a residue on your dyed fabric.

It helps to stretch your fabric and tape it to your work surface with painter's tape before marking.

Using Stencils

When marking your design with a stencil, place it on top of the fabric and tape down the top of it. Mark or draw through the stencil openings onto the fabric with a water-soluble marker.

Carefully lift the bottom of the stencil to check that you have transferred all the stencil markings before moving the stencil to continue marking your pattern.

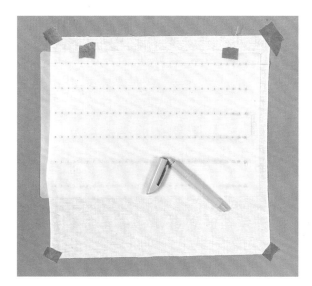
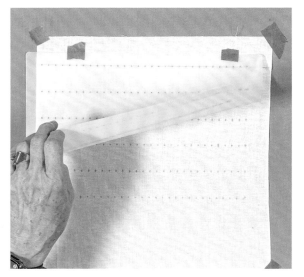

When moving the stencil to the next section of fabric to be marked, be sure to overlap by one line of stitching to be certain that your design will be consistent and accurate. Tape the stencil down again and keep marking. Continue until you have the entire design marked on the fabric.

To adapt a quilting stencil, you need to mark the design onto your fabric as it is on the stencil. Quilting stencils have bridges on the stencil that result in open areas along the stitching lines. Carefully fill in these gaps so you have continuous stitching lines.

Tracing

If you are using preprinted designs, you can trace them directly onto the fabric. If your fabric is thin enough to see through, you can tape the design to the table, layer the fabric on top, and then trace it with a water-soluble marker.

If you can't see your design easily through your fabric, tape the design and fabric to a lightbox or window to make it easier to trace.

GETTING READY TO STITCH

Now that your design is marked on your fabric, it is time to stitch!

Threading and Knotting Your Needle

When stitching, it is important to thread your needle with a doubled length of thread and to tie a large knot. This helps prevent threads from breaking or pulling the knot through the fabric, which is important to a successful design.

1. Thread your needle with a double length of bonded nylon thread.

2. Bring both ends of the thread together and place them on the index finger of your nondominant hand.

3. Place the needle on top of the threads, perpendicular to them.

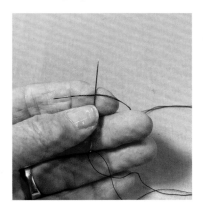

4. Pinch lightly with your thumb.

5. Wrap the working side of the thread that is under the needle around the needle point about 4 times.

6. Pinch the wraps lightly with your thumb. Then, pull the needle slowly through the wrapped

threads, keeping your finger and thumb in place.

7. You should now have a large knot at the free end of the thread. No loops of thread should be sticking out around the knot. If there are loops, grab the two threads separately and pull them until the loops disappear.

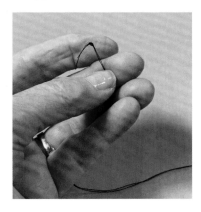

Using Buffers

When stitching designs into your fabric, you place a knot at both ends of your stitched lines to hold them in place. When you pull the threads to gather the fabric before dyeing, each knot can leave a small round white dot on the fabric. If you do not want that little white spot, you can use a *buffer*, a small folded square of fabric to place between your beginning and ending knots and your fabric surface to prevent the knot circles from showing on finished fabrics. Buffers are also helpful when stitching loosely woven fabrics, to keep the knots from pulling through the fabric.

To make and use buffers, you will need scraps of tightly woven fabrics:

1. Cut squares that are approximately 1″ × 1″ (2.5 × 2.5cm).

2. Fold in half twice.

3. Before you begin stitching your design, stitch through one buffer.

4. Stitch the line and pull the buffer snug between the knot and the beginning stitch.

5. When you are finished with a line of stitching, stitch through another buffer, moving it against the fabric.

6. When gathering your stitches prior to dyeing, be sure that both buffers remain snug against the fabric before you tie the final knot.

Basic Running Stitch

A basic running stitch is used for many shibori stitched designs. It is simple to do: Push the threaded needle down into the fabric (A) and come up in the fabric a distance away from where you went down (B); place the needle down into the fabric again, leaving about the same amount of space as you did for the first stitch (C); continue stitching up and down across the fabric.

If the stitch length and the space between the stitches is about the same, it is referred to as an even running stitch. If you vary the stitch length or the size of the spaces between stitches, it is called a random running stitch. The size and regularity of the stitches will affect the look of the final design.

Stitching the Design

Here are a few important things to know before you begin stitching:

1. Always use doubled thread.

2. Start with enough thread on the needle to finish a line of stitching or a design element. You should not start over with a new thread in the middle of a line of stitches.

3. Finish all stitching before pulling the thread (with a few exceptions, which are stated in the stitching instructions for specific techniques).

If the element you are stitching is a continuous line of stitches—for example, an edge-to-edge design comprising row after row of running stitches—start at the top line of stitches. If you are right-handed, begin stitching on the right, and vice versa if you are left-handed.

Begin with a knot and, if desired, a buffer and stitch all the way across your first line of stitches. If you want, end by stitching through a buffer and then leave at least a 4″ (10.2cm) tail of thread. Do not place a knot.

Move on to your next row of stitches and repeat until all rows are stitched. If you are stitching a smaller element that has a starting and ending point that are not the same, follow this same process.

If the design or design element you are stitching is a continuous element, meaning that it has the same starting and ending point (such as a circle, a square, or even something organic, such as a flower outline), you would choose a point on the design element to begin stitching.

Begin with a knot and, if desired, a buffer and stitch all the way around your design element. If you wish, end with a buffer and leave at least a 4″ tail of thread. Do not place a knot.

Move on to your next element and repeat until all elements are stitched. Wherever possible, try to choose a beginning point that is closest to the edge of the design, to make it easier when it comes time to gather your threads.

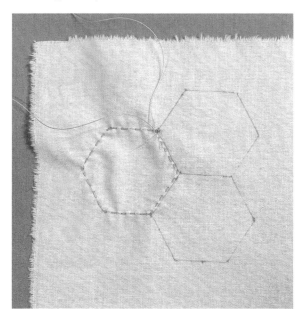

If you are stitching a complicated design, first examine the design carefully. Determine which portions of the design can be stitched as a whole element (one with the same starting and stopping point) and which portions will need to be stitched as continuous lines of stitches.

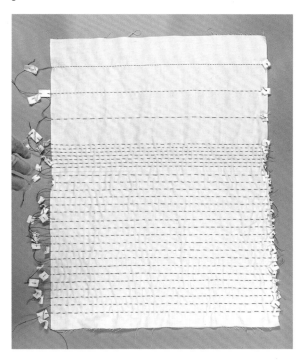

In this design, I found it easiest to stitch the center circle first, as a continuous element, and then stitch each concentric ring of scallops as its own continuous element.

For this design, I stitched the scrolled portions of the design as continuous lines, starting and stopping at two different points. Next, I stitched the outline of the continuous element of four connected leaf shapes. Finally, I stitched the echoes of each leaf shape as continuous design elements, starting and stopping at the same point each time.

Gathering the Stitching

Now that you have stitched your design, it is time to pull the threads to gather your fabric in preparation for dyeing.

EXCEPTIONS

In most of the stitched resist techniques, the designs are completely stitched before pulling the stitches. However, there will be some exceptions, such as the guntai (page 70) technique. Design instructions indicate when this is the case and explain when and how to pull the stitching.

In most cases, begin at the top of the design and partially pull two or three threads about a fourth of the way across the design to begin gathering the fabric. Move to the next two or three threads and pull those about a fourth of the way across the design. Continue down the piece until all the stitching has been partially gathered.

Move back to the top and pull more on each thread to gather more of the fabric. Continue in this manner until all the threads are pulled as much as possible and the fabric is gathered tightly. If you are using buffers, be sure that they are snug against the fabric.

Starting at the top, wet the gathered area with a spray bottle. The water allows the fabric to compress even more tightly, so now pull the threads just a bit more tightly. Tie each thread off with a double knot. This technique creates the most tension on the gathers, resulting in a crisp design.

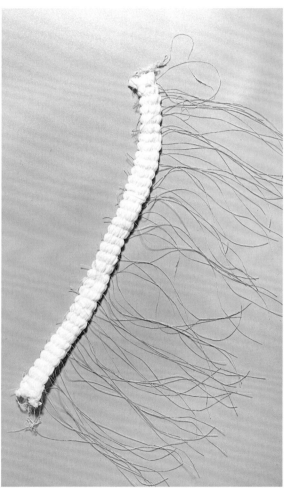

NUI SHIBORI DESIGNS

Nui shibori designs are simple yet beautiful, using basic running stitches in a variety of ways. These designs range from lovely all-over designs to geometric patterns and even intricate flowers.

HIRA-NUI

Hira-nui are lines of simple running stitches. Varying the size and placement of the stitches can yield different results. A single line of small running stitches results in a line of small white dots on a blue background. Taking longer stitches in a single row results in what looks like small V shapes. Making long, very irregular stitches results in large irregular V shapes.

1. Beginning at the top, mark horizontal lines across your fabric. Place these lines as close together or as far apart as you wish. They can be regularly spaced or random.

2. Stitch across each marked line, using buffers if desired.

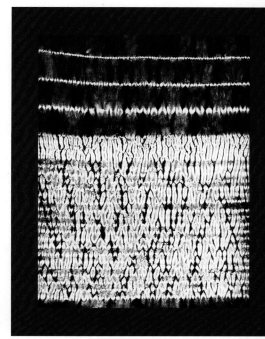

From top to bottom: lines of small, medium, and large stitches, and a group of repeated lines of stitches

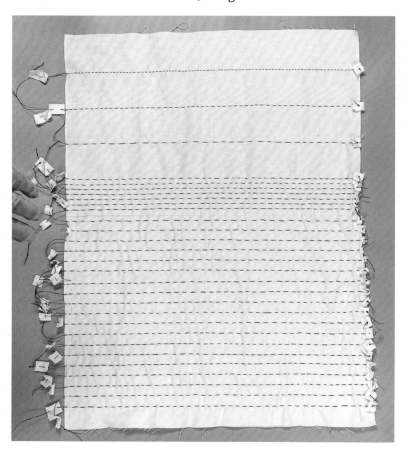

3. Follow the instructions in Gathering the Stitching (page 59). Next, follow the instructions in How to Dye in the Vat (page 30) to dye, rinse, and finish your fabric.

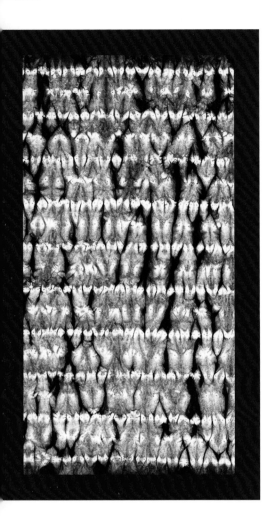

MOKUME (WOODGRAIN)

Multiple rows of randomly placed and closely spaced running stitches result in a design resembling woodgrain. It is so simple but so striking.

Mark the stitching lines about ½″ (1.3cm) apart and stitch very irregular stitches, some long and some short. Follow the instructions in Gathering the Stitching (page 59).

Follow the instructions in How to Dye in the Vat (page 30) to dye, rinse, and finish your fabric.

HAPPY ACCIDENTS

If you accidentally miss a line of stitching or one of your threads breaks prior to dyeing, all is not lost. You can simply proceed with dyeing and see what happens!

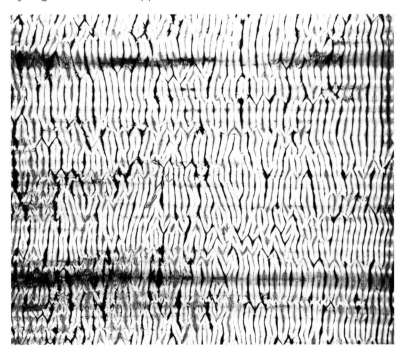

ZIGZAG

A crisp, recognizable zigzag design of white bars is created in horizontal rows, but for it to appear as a perfect zigzag, you need to follow a few specific steps:

1. Mark your fabric with a shibori zigzag stencil (see Resources, page 128) or make a vertical column of dots ½″ (1.3cm) apart with a water-soluble marker and a ruler. I marked 11 dots vertically.

2. Move the ruler to the right ¼″ (6mm) and mark the next vertical row of dots parallel to the first row.

3. Move the ruler to the right ¼″ (6mm) and mark a row of dots starting ¼″ (6mm) down from the first two rows. Always mark 11 vertical dots.

4. Continue moving the ruler to the right ¼″ (6mm) and starting each row of dots ¼″ (6mm) down from the previous row. Do this until you have 11 dots in each row at a 45° angle.

5. The twelfth row of dots will be ¼″ (6mm) away and parallel to the previous row.

6. The next row will be ¼″ (6mm) to the right and ¼″ (6mm) up from the previous row. Continue in this manner until you have 11 dots going up at a 45° angle.

7. The next row will be parallel to the previous row, and then you'll start going down again. You can make the zigzag design as wide as you want and vary the height by adding or subtracting rows of dots.

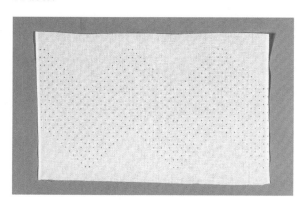

8. To achieve the parallel rows of lines in the final project, alternate beginning each line on the top and then the bottom of the fabric when you start stitching each line of dots. Begin stitching the first row with the knot on the top of your fabric. Bring your needle down through the first dot and come up through the next dot. Continue stitching across the row of dots.

9. Begin the next line of stitches with the knot on the bottom of the fabric. Bring your needle up from the underside through the first dot and back down through the fabric and through the next dot. Continue stitching across the second row of dots.

10. Alternating between beginning your rows of stitches with the knot on top and on bottom, continue to stitch the remaining rows of zigzag dots. As you add stitched lines, you will see lines of thread arranged in a diagonal pattern.

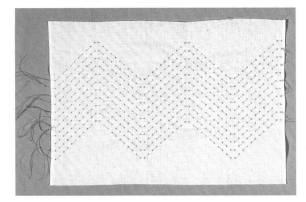

CHECK YOUR WORK!

As you work, when you come to either the top or bottom point of the zigzag, there will be two dots directly across from each other horizontally. As you add lines of stitching, the thread between those two horizontal dots will alternate between the thread being on the top of the fabric or the bottom. It is very important that those threads alternate on every line of stitching. As you add each line of stitching, carefully check that your points are alternating. If you come to a place where the stitches at the top or bottom of a zigzag will be on the same side as that same stitch on the previous line, then you have made a mistake. Carefully check your stitches. You may have missed a stitch or started on the wrong side of the fabric.

11. Pull your threads to gather the fabric, following the instructions in Gathering the Stitching (page 59). As you pull the threads, you will see diagonal folds being created. Work carefully to keep those folds as crisp as possible. The fold will change direction as you come to each top and bottom point.

12. Follow the instructions in How to Dye in the Vat (page 30) to dye, rinse, and finish your fabric.

ZIGZAG VARIATION 1

For a recognizable but more ad hoc zigzag, follow the main zigzag instructions but with one twist:

1. Mark your fabric following Steps 1–7 of the Zigzag (page 63) design.

2. When you start to stitch each line, always begin with the knot on the top.

3. Be sure that each line of stitches is identical. Follow the instructions in Gathering the Stitching (page 59).

4. Follow the instructions in How to Dye in the Vat (page 30) to dye, rinse, and finish your fabric.

ZIGZAG VARIATION 2

For a recognizable but thinner zigzag, change how you mark your fabric and sew an irregular running stitch:

1. Mark 2 vertical columns of 11 parallel dots ½˝ (1.3cm) apart.

2. Make your next dot 2½˝ (6.4cm) to the right and 3½˝ (8.9cm) up, creating a 45° angle.

3. Starting with the dot you just made, mark a vertical column of 11 dots ½˝ (1.3cm) apart. Mark a second row of dots parallel to the previous row.

4. Make your next dot 2½˝ (6.4cm) to the right and 3½˝ (8.9cm) down, creating a 45° angle.

5. Starting with the dot you just made, mark a vertical column of 11 dots ½˝ (1.3cm) apart. Mark a second row of dots parallel to the previous row. Continue in this manner until the zigzag is as wide as you prefer.

6. With a water-soluble marker and a ruler, connect the dots from the bottom of rows to the top rows at 45° angles.

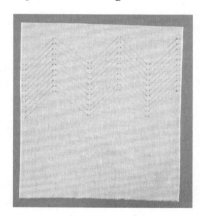

7. Be sure to make all lines of stitches with an irregular running stitch.

8. Follow the instructions in Gathering the Stitching (page 59). Next, follow the instructions in How to Dye in the Vat (page 30) to dye, rinse, and finish your fabric.

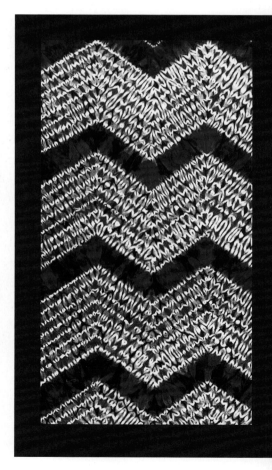

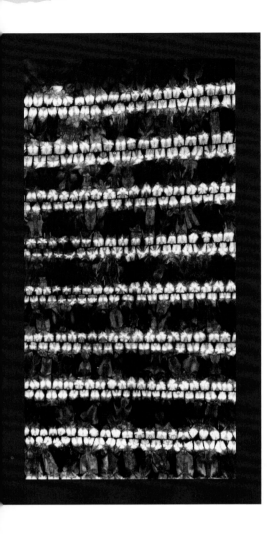

ORI-NUI

The ori-nui design uses a line of stitches made along a single fold in your fabric. You can include multiple folds and lines of stitches.

1. Draw a line where the fold (the center of the design) will be.

2. Fold the fabric at the drawn line.

3. Make a line of ¼″ (6mm) running stitches about ¼″ (6mm) away from the fold. Vary the look by varying the length of the stitches and how close they are to the fold.

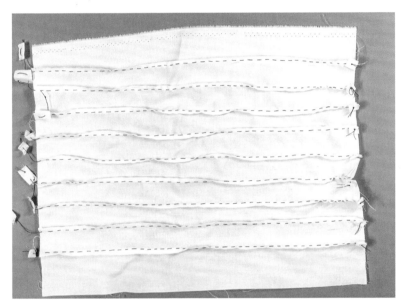

4. Follow the instructions in Gathering the Stitching (page 59). Next, follow the instructions in How to Dye in the Vat (page 30) to dye, rinse, and finish your fabric.

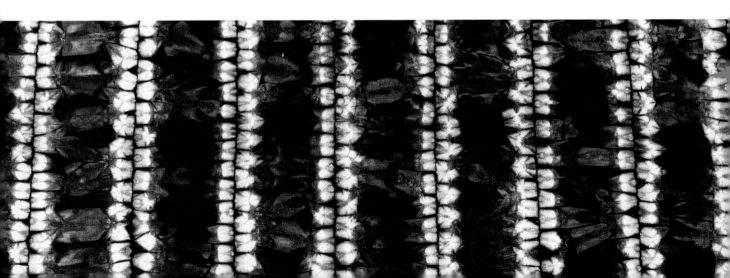

AWASE ORI-NUI

This design takes the ori-nui variation one step further. It consists of sets of parallel lines.

1. Draw 3 parallel lines spaced about ½″ (1.3cm) apart.

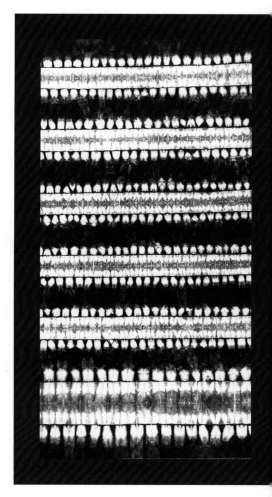

2. Bring the 2 outside lines together, with the middle line in the valley between the 2 outside lines, to create 4 layers of fabric.

3. Stitch with a medium to long running stitch through all 4 layers, about ¼″ (6mm) away from the folds.

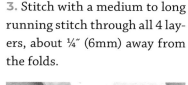

4. Follow the instructions in Gathering the Stitching (page 59). Next, follow the instructions in How to Dye in the Vat (page 30) to dye, rinse, and finish your fabric.

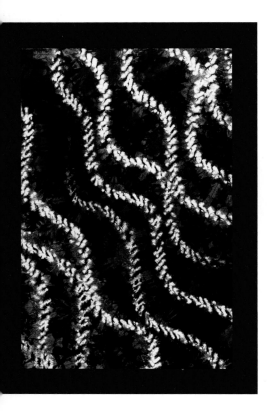

MAKI-NUI

Maki-nui is the process of stitching over a fold. This design uses a whipstitch rather than a running stitch. Your stitched lines can be straight or curved.

Whipstitch

To create a whipstitch through a fold of fabric, begin on the side of one fold, near the edge of the fabric. Bring your needle through all layers of the fabric fold, approximately ¼″ (6mm) down from the edge of the fold.

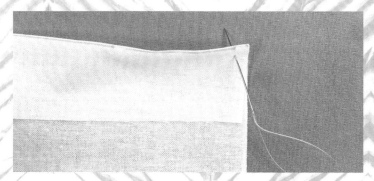

Move your needle over the fabric fold and then push again through the fabric fold, about ¼″ (6mm) away from where you placed your first stitch.

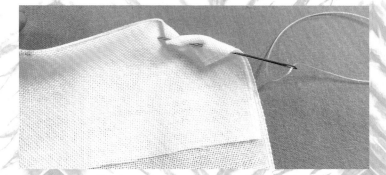

Continue to bring your thread over the fold and then through the fold until you have completed your line of stitching.

1. Draw a line or lines horizontally across your fabric. Your lines can be parallel or curved and evenly or randomly spaced.

2. Beginning with 1 line, fold the fabric along the line.

3. Whipstitch along the fold.

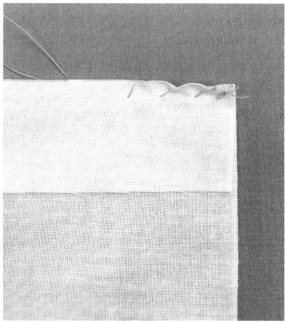

4. Repeat for the remaining drawn lines.

5. Follow the instructions in Gathering the Stitching (page 59). Next, follow the instructions in How to Dye in the Vat (page 30) to dye, rinse, and finish your fabric.

STITCH PLACEMENT

You can vary the size and placement of your stitches to create different effects. Your stitches can be farther than ¼˝ (6mm) from the fold and farther apart than ¼˝ (6mm), but don't make your stitches shorter or narrower, or you will have trouble gathering them before dyeing.

GUNTAI

Guntai, meaning "military" in Japanese, is used to create individual, more organic shapes. Guntai allows you to add delicate yet distinct motifs to your fabric by gathering the fabric tightly **as you stitch**.

1. Draw the design to be stitched. Your design can be a single shape, or it can have additional lines within the shape.

2. Take the threaded needle down through one side of the design and bring it up on the other side of the design. Again, take your needle down through the opposite side of the design. You should now have a loop of thread on top of your design.

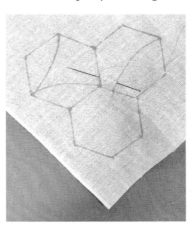

3. Pull the stitch tightly. Carefully manipulate the pleat you just formed. Push your pleats to one side or to the center as you pull each stitch

tightly. Where the top of the pleats shows under the threads will be blue in the final design. The area of fabric inside the pleats will remain undyed.

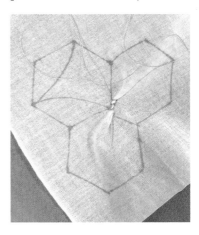

4. Repeat until the design or portion of the design is stitched.

5. Follow the instructions in How to Dye in the Vat (page 30) to dye, rinse, and finish your fabric.

MAKIAGE

Makiage designs allow you to greatly control the finished shape. This technique is often used for organic designs, such as a flower, leaf, or other natural shape. In addition to stitching around your chosen shape, you wrap your fabric to create the design.

1. Draw your chosen shape.

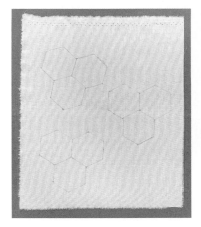

2. Make small running stitches around the perimeter of your shape.

3. Pull the stitches very tightly and tie a knot.

4. Beginning at your line of pulled stitches, tightly wrap the protruding fabric with thread. Wrap to the top of your shape and then back down. Tie a knot.

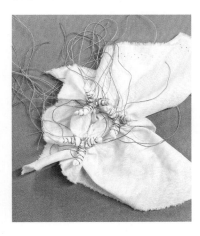

5. Follow the instructions in How to Dye in the Vat (page 30) to dye, rinse, and finish your fabric.

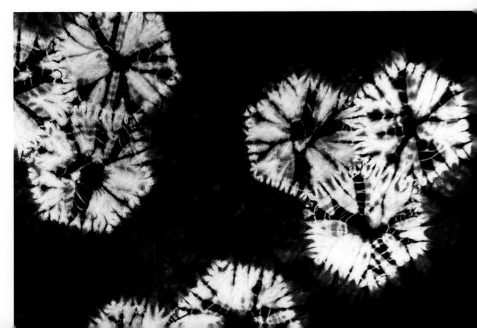

KUMO

Kumo, meaning "spider" in Japanese, is also sometimes referred to as "spider tie-dye" due to the resulting motifs sometime resembling spider webs. In this technique, sections of cloth are pinched to form a cone and then wrapped with thread or string to resist the dye. This technique is very similar to kanoko (see page 49) shibori, except the pinched fabric is wrapped with thread to create a very subtle spiral effect rather than individual rings.

1. Choose where you want your design to appear and pinch the fabric.

2. Beginning at the bottom of the pinched section, tightly wrap the pinched section of fabric with thread or string from bottom to top, and then from top to bottom.

3. Tie a knot to secure the wrapped section. You can add additional wrapped sections, which can be placed very close together, to change the look of the final design.

4. Follow the instructions in How to Dye in the Vat (page 30) to dye, rinse, and finish your fabric.

You can create multiples of this motif, or you can make one single kumo design on your fabric.

MIURA

Miura shibori creates a distinct all-over pattern of irregular circular motifs. In miura, the process of looping and binding small snippets of fabric creates the pattern. Practitioners use a long, hooked needle, secured to a stable object, to retain tension as the fabric is gathered and stitched. To find a miura needle, see the Resources (page 128). I use cotton thread to do this wrapping because it is not slick and holds better.

1. Secure your needle to a stable object, such as a special stand, or hang it from a cord on a C-clamp hooked to a table. The needle needs to hang free so it can be moved and hooked on the fabric as you progress with the design.

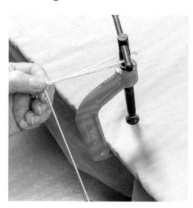

2. Work from one corner of the fabric toward the opposite corner (on the bias). Secure your thread to your fabric by wrapping and tying off one corner. Hook that corner onto your needle. Drape an area of the fabric near that corner over the tip of your index finger. Wrap thread in a clockwise direction around the protruding fabric.

3. Hook the needle into the top of the wrapped fabric, where your fingernail is. While retaining tension on your thread, pull down on your fabric to make a tightly bound circle.

4. Select another section of fabric very close to the section you just bound. Repeat Steps 2–3 to create another bound circle. Continue in this manner until all your fabric is bound. Remember, the tension between the needle and the thread, coupled with the close placement of the circles, keeps the stitching tight. The circles can be small or large but are traditionally very close together.

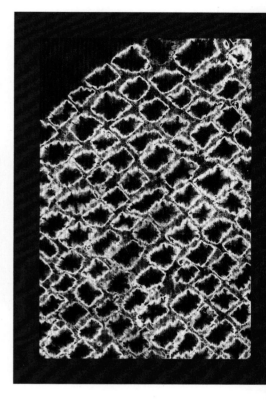

5. Follow the instructions in How to Dye in the Vat (page 30) to dye, rinse, and finish your fabric.

KARAMATSU (JAPANESE LARCH)

Also called the Japanese larch, the karamatsu design consists of a series of concentric circles stitched and pulled separately. A row can include one circle or multiple circles. These steps demonstrate how to create several rows of karamatsu motifs:

1. Decide the finished size of your karamatsu circles. The circles in this example are 2˝ (5.1cm) in diameter. Draw horizontal lines across your fabric, leaving room between the rows. I spaced mine a half circle apart, so I drew a horizontal line every 3˝ (7.6cm).

2. Place a dot where you want your first circle to begin. Mark another dot where the circle will end, in this case 2˝ (5.1cm) farther along the line. Mark the center of the circle. Move 2˝ (5.1cm) farther down your line and mark your second circle, and then move another 2˝ (5.1cm) and mark the third circle. Repeat for the remaining horizontal lines.

3. This design comprises concentric circles. Draw a semicircle template the size of your finished circle on lightweight cardboard or template plastic. Create additional semicircle templates, each one smaller than the last. In the example, I used 3 semicircle templates. You can also use a circle template that has multiple sizes.

4. With the templates you just created and the dots you made in Step 2, mark your semicircles onto your fabric above the horizontal line.

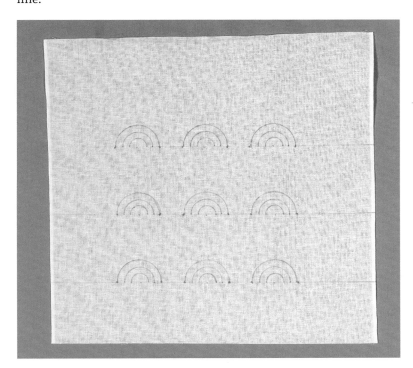

You can also offset lines of smaller circles for additional visual interest.

5. Fold your fabric along each marked horizontal line. Begin and end your lines of stitching by using buffers if you do not want the knot circles to show. Stitch the first marked semicircle through both layers of fabric. Carry the thread to the next motif and stitch the same concentric circle. Continue in this manner across the fabric until the first line of semicircles is stitched.

6. Rethread your needle and begin on the next concentric circle, again stitching through both layers of fabric. Carry the thread to the next motif and stitch. Continue in this manner until each row is stitched.

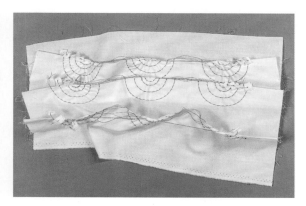

7. Pull your threads by following the instructions in Gathering the Stitching (page 59).

8. Follow the instructions in How to Dye in the Vat (page 30) to dye, rinse, and finish your fabric.

To create one large karamatsu design, follow the steps above, but only mark and stitch one large semicircle.

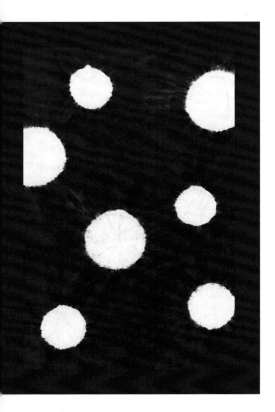

BOUSHI (CAPPED DESIGNS)

In traditional boushi, a part of the fabric is covered, or *capped*, so that the capped portion remains undyed and only the background is dyed in indigo. The capped portion of the fabric can be a certain shape or design, or it can simply be a section of the cloth from edge to edge.

Below, I explain how to cap a circular design, but you can follow these steps to cap any shape:

1. Make a running stitch around the outline of the section of fabric to be capped.

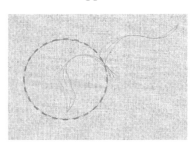

2. Gently pull the thread to gather the fabric. Do not pull the gathers very tightly. Manipulate the fabric above and below the stitching to form soft gathers, but not so tightly as to create hard pleats.

3. Select a plug, usually a dowel, a cork, or a tight roll of newspaper. Wrap the plug in plastic wrap and insert it into the gathered area. Pull the threads you stitched the motif with a bit more tightly, being sure that your gathers are even and that

no sections overlap. Tie off the bundle around the plug.

4. Use a very lightweight vinyl or plastic wrap to cover, or *cap*, the plugged area. When you cover the area, work the plastic against the plug with tiny gathers, not large pleats. You do not want any gaps where dye could enter your capped section. Wrap around the bottom of the capped area very tightly with a length of heavier-weight thread, just below the original stitching.

5. Pull all the loose ends of your vinyl or plastic wrap up over the capped area so that you have no extra bits of plastic that could interfere with the dye. Wrap the ends against the capped area with heavy thread. Wrap from bottom to top and back down. Tie a knot. To check your work, turn the piece upside down. You should not see any of your original threads hanging down below the capping.

6. Follow the instructions in How to Dye in the Vat (page 30) to dye, rinse, and finish your fabric.

Traditional Plugs

The traditional Japanese plug is made by rolling wet newspaper very tightly to make a firm cylindrical shape. Keep adding layers of wet newspaper until the plug is the size you need for the design. To successfully make this item, follow these steps:

1. Wet a double sheet of newspaper in a tub of water. Do not soak it for a long time—just dip it to wet it thoroughly.

2. Fold the wet paper in half lengthwise and repeat until your folded stack is approximately 2½″ to 3″ (6.4–7.6cm) wide.

3. Beginning on one short end, fold over a small portion and start rolling. Press down firmly on the paper as you roll.

4. Keep adding layers of wet paper until the roll is as large as you want. It should be compressed and very firm.

5. To cover the entire plug with a thin piece of plastic wrap, start at one end with the roll on top of the plastic, roll it a few times, fold both sides of the plastic wrap toward the center, and then continue to roll to the end of the plastic wrap.

6. Push down and roll back and forth to compress the roll as much as you can.

7. Wrap the plug with sewing thread to hold everything together.

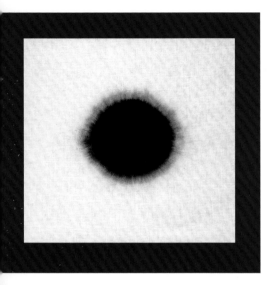

SAKA-BOUSHI

The opposite of boushi, in saka-boushi the background rather than the area inside the stitched design is covered in plastic to resist the indigo. After you stitch around the perimeter of your design, wrap and cap the background fabric instead of the area inside each design.

Follow the instructions in How to Dye in the Vat (page 30) to dye, rinse, and finish your fabric.

HINODE (CIRCLE SUNRISE)

After dyeing, *hinode* results in white circle outlines on a blue background. The design is a series of rows of half circles that are stitched and pulled tightly before dyeing. The circles can be any size you choose, but the effect is best when the rows and the half circles are spaced a full circle diameter apart, and every other row of circles is offset.

1. Decide the finished size of your circles. This example features 1½″ (3.8cm) circles. Create a 1½″ (3.8cm) half-circle template out of template plastic or cardboard.

2. Starting the first line 2″ (5.1cm) below the top of the fabric to allow space for the design, draw parallel lines 1½″ (3.8cm) apart across your fabric.

3. Trace semicircles across the first line, leaving 1½″ (3.8cm) between each half circle.

4. On the next line, starting ¼″ (6mm) from the edge, trace semicircles across the line, spacing them 1½″ (3.8cm) apart. Repeat Steps 4–5 for all lines.

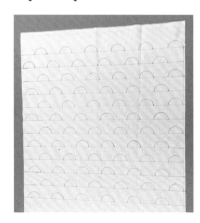

5. Fold the fabric along each horizontal line and make small running stitches around the first semicircle. Carry your thread to the next semicircle and stitch. Continue until you have stitched the full row of semicircles. Do not stitch between the motifs. Repeat for each line of half circles.

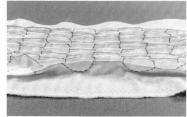

6. Before pulling the stitching, count the number of half circles in each row. Pull the stitches, gathering the threads. The circles will protrude from the line of stitches.

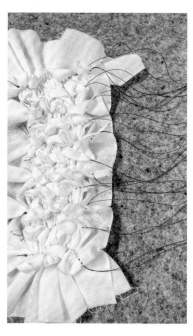

7. Count the number of circles again to be sure that the correct number of circles is protruding. It is easy for a circle to get caught in the stitching. If that happens, pull the circle out.

Notice that the second circle on the top edge is folded inward and does not protrude from the fabric.

Rows of circles after the folded-down circle was released

8. Follow the instructions in How to Dye in the Vat (page 30) to dye, rinse, and finish your fabric.

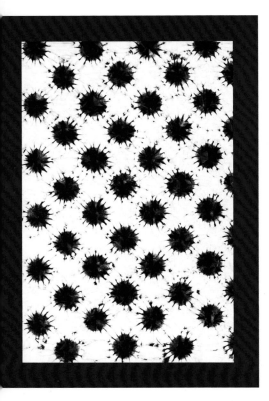

HINODE GOMU (REVERSE SUNRISE)

The initial design is the same as with hinode, but the background is wrapped, so the fabric remains almost white with blue circles.

1. Follow the instructions for Hinode (Circle Sunrise), page 78.

2. Wrap heavy yarn very tightly between the rows of circles and very close to the circles. Place the yarn wraps very close together.

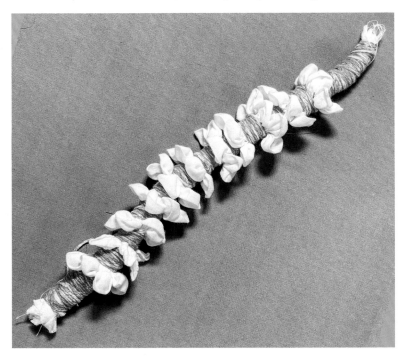

3. Follow the instructions in How to Dye in the Vat (page 30) to dye, rinse, and finish your fabric.

HINODE VARIATION 1

After dyeing, the result is an all-over pattern of white circles featuring a spider web–like design on a blue background.

1. Follow the instructions for Hinode (Circle Sunrise), page 78.

2. Before dyeing, wrap each of the protruding circles with thread from bottom to top and back down again.

3. Follow the instructions in How to Dye in the Vat (page 30) to dye, rinse, and finish your fabric.

HINODE VARIATION 2

After dyeing, the result is blue circles on a mottled blue and white background.

1. Follow the instructions for Hinode (Circle Sunrise), page 78.

2. Before dyeing, wrap thread, not yarn, very tightly between the rows of circles.

3. Wrap very close to the circles and place the thread wraps fairly far apart.

4. Wrap in one direction on a diagonal and then back diagonally in the other direction.

5. Follow the instructions in How to Dye in the Vat (page 30) to dye, rinse, and finish your fabric.

KATANO

The repeated all-over Katano design is created by evenly pleating your fabric before marking and stitching the design. The crisp design is achieved by sandwiching your main fabric piece between two sacrificial pieces of fabric that will absorb some of the dye and show the stitching lines, leaving the middle layer with clean lines.

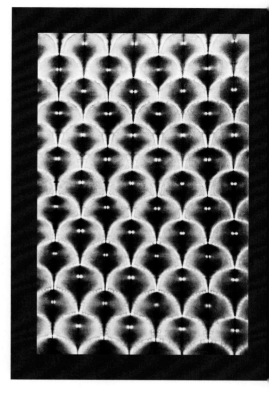

1. On your first piece of fabric, mark a horizontal line of dots, spaced 1½˝ (3.8cm) apart. Add a second, identical horizontal line of dots 1½˝ (3.8cm) down from the previous line. Continue in this manner until your entire piece of fabric is marked.

2. On each marked line, using the dots as your guide, make a very small stitch, picking up only 2 or 3 threads at the first dot. Skip the second dot. Make your next very small stitch at the third dot, again picking up only 2 or 3 threads. Continue across the fabric, making tiny stitches at every other dot.

4. Turn the piece over. On the top marked line, make tiny stitches at the dots you skipped on the front side.

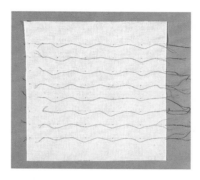

5. Slowly pull the threads on the front side and then on the back side. Pleats will start to form in the fabric.

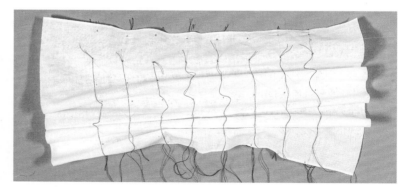

6. Tie the threads on each side to stabilize the pleats. These threads do not need to be tied very tightly. Repeat Steps 1–6 for the remaining 2 pieces of fabric.

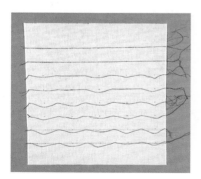

3. Repeat Step 2 along each marked line.

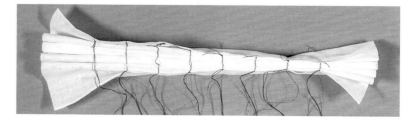

7. After the pleats are formed, on the pleated fabric bundle that will be your top piece, draw your desired design on the top pleat. The design you draw will be replicated through all layers of all 3 bundles of your pleated fabric. You can draw your design freehand or make a small template to ensure an even design across your fabric. For this example, I made a curved template the same width as the pleated fabric.

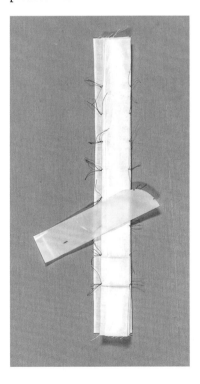

8. Continue marking along the full length of your pleated fabric. In this example, I marked the curve on the fabric and then turned the template over, lined it up with the previous curve, and marked it again. I then went back and marked a small dot where I wanted to stitch over the edge of the pleats for a small resist between the large curved areas.

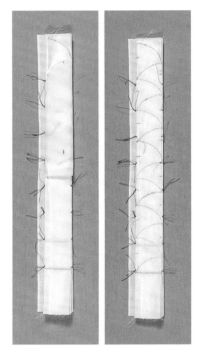

STAB STITCH
Stab stitches are made by bringing the needle down through your fabric and back up again at a perpendicular angle to the fabric. Your stitches cannot be angled, and only one stitch is made at a time.

BACKSTITCH
1. To create a backstitch, take your needle down through all layers of your fabic.

2. Bring your needle back up through your fabric 1 stitch length away from your first stitch.

3. Take your needle back down through your initial stitch hole.

4. Bring your needle back up through your fabric 2 stitch lengths away from the end point of your first stitch.

5. Take your needle back down through your second needle hole and continue in this manner.

9. Stab stitch with a sturdy needle into the side of the fold, and then go over the fold and stab again. Continue to stab stitch your design through all layers of fabric. Remember, your stitches need to be straight up and down through all layers of fabric and not at an angle. When securing your first stitch, stitch around and through the layers of the bundle to wrap them all, ensuring a continuous design. If you want a break in the center of your design, do not loop all the layers to secure them.

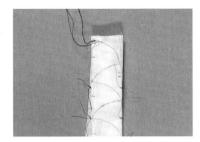

10. Follow the instructions in How to Dye in the Vat (page 30) to dye, rinse, and finish your fabric.

HOTARU (FIREFLY)

Characterized by hazy white circles on a blue background, this design is reminiscent of fireflies at night. The hazy white circles are made by sandwiching the fabric between two dense flat balls of cotton held in place by buttons or pieces of cardboard stitched in the fabric.

In addition to the typical supplies, to create this design, you'll need cotton batting and two buttons or pieces of lightweight cardboard per firefly.

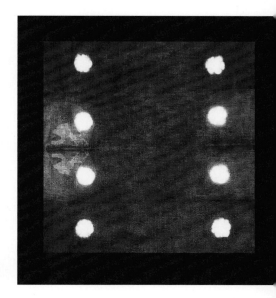

1. Cut 2 squares 4″ × 4″ (10.2 × 10.2cm) of cotton batting for each firefly. Fold each corner of your batting square to the center.

2. Fold each corner in again to create a dense cotton blob, approximately 1″ (2.5cm) in diameter.

3. Wrap heavy thread around the bundle, flatten it, and tie it off, creating a very dense disk.

4. Repeat to make as many disks as you need. Remember, it takes 2 disks to make 1 firefly.

5. Sandwich the fabric between 2 cotton disks, one on either side of the fabric. Place buttons or small scraps of cardboard on the outsides of your cotton disks and stitch through the bundles to secure them. Stitch back and forth through the buttons and cotton balls several times, pulling very tightly, and tie them off.

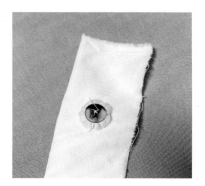

6. Follow the instructions in How to Dye in the Vat (page 30) to dye, rinse, and finish your fabric.

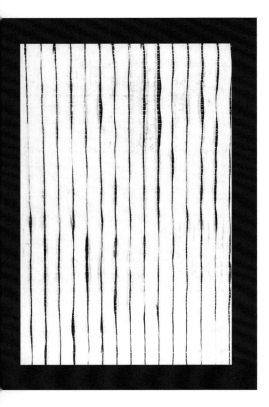

TESUJI

Tesuji shibori results in a mostly white fabric with occasional blue vertical streaks.

In addition to the typical supplies, you will need a clean length of rubber or plastic hose, such as a garden hose.

1. Draw a horizontal line across your fabric.

2. Mark dots every ⅜″ (1cm) along your line. Create an identical line of dots 1½″ (3.8cm) below the first row. Continue adding lines and dots until the entire piece of fabric is marked.

USE A PLEATING STENCIL

To make your marking go more quickly, use a template. To find the template I use, go to the Resources (page 128). Line up a row of dots along the line to keep your marks straight across the fabric. Keep the stencil in the correct place with a few small pieces of blue tape. Mark your fabric with a water-soluble marker.

As you move the stencil across the fabric, line up the previous dots and the line you drew to keep everything straight. When you finish marking one set of dots, line up the top row of dots on the stencil with the bottom row of dots you have already marked. Remember to retape the stencil before you continue to mark, or it may move. Continue marking the dots until the entire piece of fabric is marked with dots.

3. Stitch each line of dots. Begin each row by stitching down through the first dot so that all of your beginning knots sit on the top of the fabric.

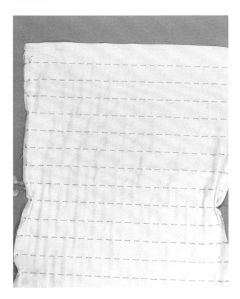

4. As you pull your stitches, you will create the pleats that make the design. Start by pulling 3 or 4 threads at a time. Gather a few inches carefully, creating very small pleats. You may need to manipulate and tug the little pleats from above and below to smooth them.

5. Move to the next 3 or 4 threads to pull up another few inches. Continue all the way down the piece and then go back to the top and pull the threads farther across the piece. Repeat this process until all the rows of stitching are pulled and small pleats have formed. Straighten the small pleats if necessary. Tie knots to finish.

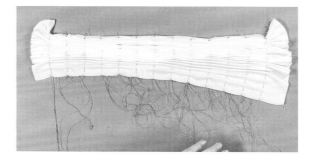

6. Place the pleated fabric along the hose, with the pleats facing out. Secure the top and bottom ends with rubber bands to hold your fabric in place.

7. Tie a new length of heavier-weight thread to the hose just above your fabric. Start wrapping the thread very tightly around the pleated bundle and the hose at ¼″–¾″ (6–19mm) intervals. The pleats will flatten as you wrap, which is okay, but try to keep the pleats facing out instead of folding to one side. When you reach the bottom, tie a knot and tape the end of the thread to the hose.

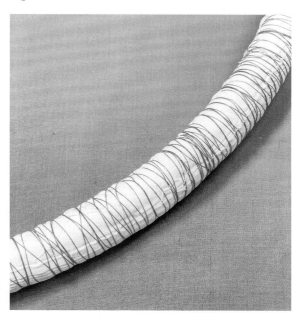

8. Follow the instructions in How to Dye in the Vat (page 30) to dye, rinse, and finish your fabric.

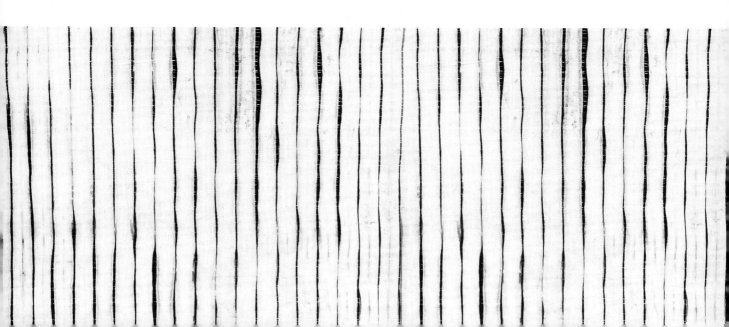

ARASHI SHIBORI

Arashi means "storm" in Japanese. To achieve these designs, fabric is wrapped diagonally around a pole and then wrapped with string to hold the fabric against the pole. The wrapped fabric is then pushed to the bottom of the pole to produce diagonal stripes that resemble rain.

The direction the fabric is wrapped and how it is bound determines the design. The design can be varied by how heavy the string is, how far apart the wraps are, whether the fabric is only wrapped once or removed and wrapped again, and other factors.

In addition to your typical supplies, you will need a pole to wrap. Pick up a length of 3″ (7.6cm) PVC pipe at least 2½′ (76.2cm) long.

Photo by C&T Publishing, Inc.

BASIC POLE WRAPPING

To make the traditional arashi pattern, follow these steps:

1. Accordion-fold your fabric lengthwise until the fabric bundle is no more than 4″ (10.2cm) wide.

2. Place the top corner of your fabric against the pole, near the top at a diagonal, and secure it with a small piece of painter's tape. Wrap your fabric around the pole diagonally, in a clockwise direction. If necessary, add additional pieces of painter's tape to secure your fabric as you work.

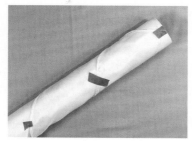

3. Secure the fabric to the pole with twine or string. Wrap the string around the fabric in the same direction you wrapped the fabric onto the pole, leaving space between each wrap. As you wrap, remove the bits of tape you used to secure the fabric. Leaving larger spaces between wraps results in more dyed area on the finished piece, while closely placed string leaves more fabric undyed.

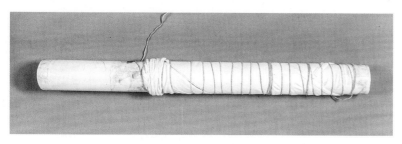

4. Compress the fabric toward the end of the pole where you started. Be careful to not push the fabric off the end of the pole. Place a few rubber bands or tape near the end of the pole to prevent pushing the fabric off the end.

5. Tie off your twine or string and tape down the ends.

6. Follow the instructions in How to Dye in the Vat (page 30) to dye, rinse, and finish your fabric.

Experiment with wrapping in different directions on folded or unfolded fabric for a variety of designs.

TINY PLEATS

Pleating your fabric as it is wrapped and compressed results in an entirely different look, slightly reminiscent of part of a cross section of a tree trunk.

1. Secure a top corner to the top of your pole with a rubber band. Add a second rubber band approximately 6˝ (15.2cm) below the first one.

2. Scrunch the fabric between the 2 rubber bands into tiny pleats. Manipulate the fabric to remove any large folds as you go. Wrap and secure the area you just pleated with a heavier-weight thread. When you reach the second rubber band, tape your string to the pole to hold it temporarily.

rubber band. Again, scrunch the fabric between the rubber bands into tiny pleats, removing any folds as you go. Secure the section you just completed and continue in this manner to pleat and secure the remaining fabric.

4. When you have about 15˝ (38.1cm) pleated, hold the string and compress the fabric toward the end of the pole where you started. Be careful to not push the fabric off the end of the pole. Place a few rubber bands or tape near the end of the pole to prevent pushing the fabric off the end.

5. Continue pleating, wrapping, and compressing until the piece is finished.

3. Move the first rubber band down to approximately 6˝ (15.2cm) below the second

6. Follow the instructions in How to Dye in the Vat (page 30) to dye, rinse, and finish your fabric.

SPECIAL FOLDING AND POLE WRAPPING

This graphic design is unlike normal itajime or arashi shibori lines because some of the lines go horizontal, some diagonal, and others vertical. It reminds me of 1930s art deco. First, you will fold the fabric in a special way not previously illustrated, and then you'll wrap it around a pole with yarn or cord.

1. Fold the fabric by using the basic accordion fold; see Five Ways to Fold the Fabric (page 36). Lay the folded fabric flat.

2. Fold 1 end of your accordion-folded strip in half lengthwise to find the center of the strip. Gently crease to mark the center.

3. Lay the piece flat again. Keep 1 corner flat on the surface. Fold the other corner to meet the center line and crease the small triangle.

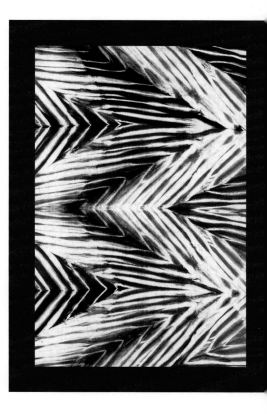

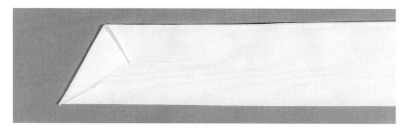

4. This triangle is what we are working with in this piece.

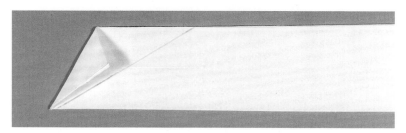

5. Turn the piece over and fold the triangle back so the small side meets the fold.

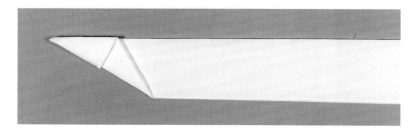

6. Bring the long tail back to meet the upper right side of the triangle.

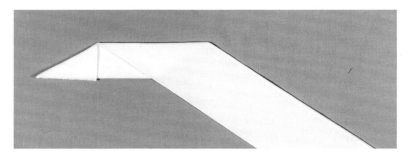

7. Bring the tail back and forth on the top side to meet the point of the previous fold, which will be under the fold. Raise the fold slightly to see the point. Keep the top-edge and bottom-edge folds even.

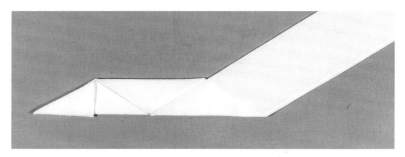

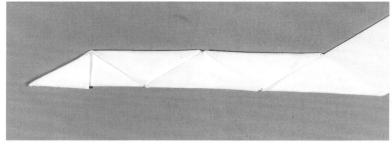

8. Hold the folds in place with small pieces of blue tape.

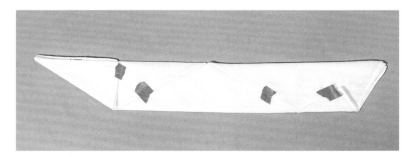

9. Carefully wrap the folded fabric right side out on the pole. Tape it in place.

10. Wrap the fabric to the pole with yarn or small cord. Place the wraps about 1″ (2.5cm) apart. Remove any tape as you come to it; do not wrap around the tape.

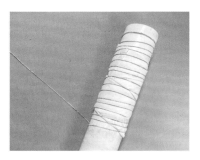

11. When you have wrapped all the fabric, push the fabric toward the end of the pole. It will form pleats between the wraps. Be careful to not push the fabric off the end of the pole.

12. The piece is ready to wet and dye. I treat this design very differently than most others by dipping it 7 or 8 times. After the dye has oxidized, I place the pole in the vat and **leave it there overnight, up to 24 hours**. Remove and allow it to oxidize for an hour, then dip it 2 or 3 more times. Let it oxidize overnight. Follow the instructions in Finishing the Fabrics (page 32).

EXTRA FUN TECHNIQUES

Photo by C&T Publishing, Inc.

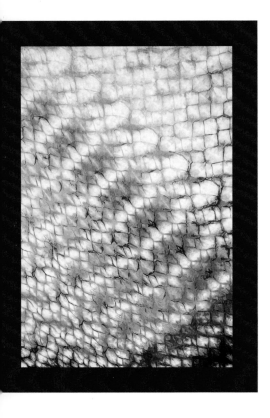

HONEYCOMB

This technique is extremely easy and results in an all-over design that looks like a honeycomb or large raindrops. It is also a gradient design that starts lighter on one side and transitions to darker on the other. You can add interest by leaving an area unwrapped.

In addition to the typical supplies, you'll need cording, ribbon, or ikat tape (a very strong yet thin tape used for a special type of weaving). For purchasing options, see Resources (page 128).

The design can be worked on the straight grain or on the bias.

1. Cut a piece of cord, ribbon, or tape a few inches longer than the widest part of the fabric to be rolled (corner to corner).

2. Move the cord to 1 corner and begin to roll the fabric around the cord.

3. Roll fairly tightly, but loosely enough for the cord to move easily. Continue to roll until you reach the opposite side. You can leave a portion unwrapped to create an edge of solid blue.

4. Hold both ends of the cord in one hand and push the fabric to the center.

5. Tie the ends of cord together in a very tight knot, compressing the fabric into a tight donut shape.

6. Follow the instructions in How to Dye in the Vat (page 30) to dye, rinse, and finish your fabric.

SPRING-TOY RESIST

This is a crazy-fun way to resist dye, and the results are different every time. Each piece is truly one of a kind. The spring-toy resist technique works best on scarves or lightweight fabrics.

In addition to the typical supplies, you will also need three pieces of strong twine, each about 15″ (38.1cm) long, and a child's spring toy, such as a Slinky. You'll also need a second set of hands, so recruit a friend or family member to help out.

1. Wet the fabric.

2. Lay the fabric flat on a table or surface, aligning the edge of the fabric with the edge of the surface.

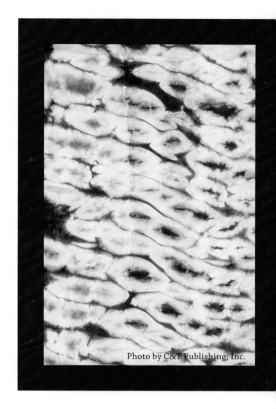

Photo by C&T Publishing, Inc.

4. Have your assistant hold the end of the spring toy upright and catch the edge of the fabric between 2 rings.

3. Smooth out any large wrinkles.

5. Pull the spring toy to the other end of the fabric, opening up the rings of the spring.

6. Gather and hold any extra rings after pulling the toy across the fabric, leaving wide spaces between them.

7. Catch the other end of the fabric between 2 rings.

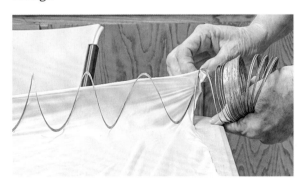

8. Hold the spring very taut on both ends, and then you and your helper roll the spring to encase it inside the fabric.

9. As your helper holds their end of the spring very taut, move toward them, gathering the fabric into the open rings of the spring toy as you go. As you gather, be sure to keep your thumbs in the center of the spring to hold a passage open from one end of the spring to the other.

10. While your helper holds the compressed spring, thread a piece of twine through the center and tie a tight knot. Repeat with the other 2 pieces of twine, spacing them evenly around the spring.

11. Follow the instructions in How to Dye in the Vat (page 30) to dye, rinse, and finish your fabric.

TWIST

This design can be blue stripes on a lot of background or light and dark blue stripes with some background. This is a great, almost solid-looking fabric for quilters to use in their quilts. It also makes a simple yet beautiful scarf.

Two people make the process easier, but if your piece of fabric is long, you can secure one end with a clamp if you don't have a helper.

1. Wet the fabric.

2. If you have an assistant, each of you hold 1 end and start to twist clockwise. If you are on your own, clamp or hold 1 end of the fabric to your work surface and begin to twist the free end clockwise.

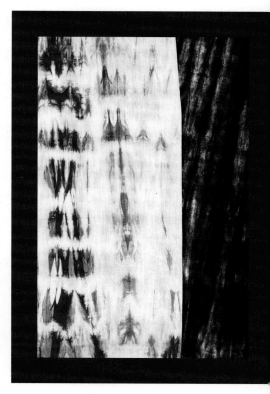

3. Continue twisting until the fabric twists back on itself. Hold the center and allow the fabric to fold back on itself, twisting in the process.

5. Follow the instructions in How to Dye in the Vat (page 30) to dye, rinse, and finish your fabric.

After dyeing, if there is too much undyed fabric for your liking, repeat the process, but this time twist the fabric in a counterclockwise direction.

4. Continue to hold the ends and twist clockwise until the fabric bundle is very tight. Force an opening in the folded center and thread the free ends of the twist into the opening to hold it all together.

SCRUNCH

This creates a beautiful, mottled effect that resembles clouds. This also makes a great filler fabric for quilting or a gorgeous simple scarf or shawl.

In addition to the typical supplies, you'll need a recycled mesh produce bag.

1. Wet your fabric and lay it out flat.

2. Start in 1 corner, with your thumbs close together and flat on the surface.

3. Start bringing the fabric toward you with your fingers, forming round folds.

4. Pull the folds toward your thumbs from all directions, grabbing just a bit of fabric at a time. Keep your hands over the gathered fabric so that it remains gathered.

5. If it becomes necessary—for example, when working with a large piece of fabric—hold the gathers with 1 hand and use the other hand to keep gathering the fabric.

6. After all the fabric is gathered, use both hands to form it into a ball.

7. Wedge it very tightly into the corner of the mesh produce bag.

8. Twist the bag to hold the fabric tight.

9. Place a rubber band around the bag, close to the fabric bundle.

10. Follow the instructions in How to Dye in the Vat (page 30) to dye, rinse, and finish your fabric. When you dye the fabric, squeeze the fabric bundle while it is submerged in the vat. The more you squeeze, the more blue the fabric will be. If you want a lot of white, do not squeeze the bundle. Squeeze the bundle tightly before removing it from the indigo vat to prevent large drips. Rinse the bundle before removing the fabric from the mesh bag.

PROJECTS

These projects are fun ways to use the beautiful fabrics you make by using the new shibori techniques you're learning. In this case, the fabric is the star.

HINODE SHOWCASE PILLOW

Finished pillow: 16″ × 16″ (40cm × 40cm)

This pillow combines all the stitched resist hinode designs and variations into one striking pillow. You will use three fat quarters for the front and one for the pillow back. You'll have hand-dyed scraps left over, which is always a good thing!

MATERIALS

Cotton fabric: 4 fat quarters

Small piece of template plastic or light cardboard

Bonded nylon or heavy nylon upholstery thread

Ruler

Water-soluble marker

Yarn to wrap stitched fabric

Blue painter's tape

Sewing thread in blue or white

Button for decoration

16″ × 16″ (40cm × 40cm) square pillow form

DYEING THE FABRICS

1. Follow the instructions in Hinode (Circle Sunrise), page 78, to dye the first fat quarter.

2. Follow the instructions in Hinode Gomu (Reverse Sunrise), page 80, to dye the second fat quarter.

3. Follow the instructions in Hinode Variation 1, page 81, to dye the third fat quarter.

4. Follow the instructions in Hinode Variation 2, page 82, to dye the fourth fat quarter.

CONSTRUCTION

Seam allowances are ¼˝ (6mm) unless otherwise stated.

1. Cut a square 16½˝ × 16½˝ (41.9 × 41.9cm) from all 4 fat quarters. Reserve the Hinode Gomu (Reverse Sunrise) fat quarter for the pillow back. This fabric has blue circles on an almost white background.

2. With right sides together, lay the Hinode Variation 2 fabric on top of the Hinode Variation 1 fabric.

3. Stitch across the top of the layered fat quarters and down 6˝ (15.2cm) along the right side.

4. Clip the top right corner and turn the fabrics right side out. Press.

5. With the Hinode Variation 2 fabric faceup, draw a line from the end of the stitching along the side to 1˝ (2.5cm) below the top right corner. Cut away the top fabric along the line, being careful to not cut the bottom fabric.

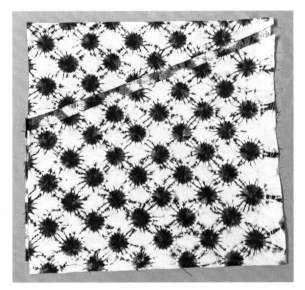

6. Place the Hinode (Circle Sunrise) fabric faceup. Layer the piece completed in Step 5 on top, with the Hinode Variation 2 fabric facedown and 2″ (5.1cm) from the top edge of the bottom fabric. Pin in place.

7. Find the starting and ending points of the cut edge of the lighter fabric that you cut in Step 5. Mark them with pins. Draw a line ½″ (1.3cm) above the marked cut edge and sew along the line you just drew.

8. Turn the piece over and cut the bottom edges even.

9. From the front side, fold the loose corner down and secure it with a decorative button.

10. Place the reserved back piece right sides together with the pillow front and sew around the pillow, using a ⅜″ (1cm) seam allowance. Leave an 8″ (20.3cm) opening at the bottom for turning.

11. Turn the pillow cover right side out. Insert the pillow form into the cover and hand stitch the opening closed.

Photo by C&T Publishing, Inc.

ZIGZAG JOY TABLE RUNNER

Finished table runner: 19″ × 42″ (48.3 × 106.7cm)

Stitched resists made with stencils create the stunning motifs on this beautiful linen table runner. Creating the designs is a piece of cake with quilting and shibori stencils.

MATERIALS

Medium-weight linen: ¾ yard (68.6cm) of 45″ (1.14m) wide

Water-soluble marker

Quilting stencil of your choice for the center design; I used the 2″ Clamshell Pyramid stencil (see Resources, page 128)

Blue painter's tape

Ruler

Bonded nylon or heavy nylon upholstery thread

Blue sewing thread

Fabric scraps to use as buffers

Optional: Shibori stencil in zigzag design (see Resources, page 128)

DYEING THE FABRICS

1. Press the fabric. Fold it in half, selvage to selvage, and press lightly. Fold again, cut edge to cut edge, and press lightly to mark the center. Unfold and lay flat. Mark the 2 lines with a water-soluble marker. Measure 5″ (12.7cm) from each short selvage edge and mark a line from long cut edge to long cut edge, perpendicular to the marked center line. This line needs to be very straight!

2. Using the lines you just drew as a guide, follow the instructions in Using Stencils (page 54) and the quilting stencil to transfer the design to the center of your fabric.

3. Following the instructions in Stitching the Design (page 57) and Gathering the Stitching (page 59), stitch and gather your center design, but do not yet dye the fabric.

4. Using the lines along the short selvage edges that you drew in Step 1, follow the instructions in Zigzag (page 63) to transfer and stitch the design to both short edges of your fabric.

5. Follow the instructions in Gathering the Stitching (page 59) to gather your edge designs.

6. Follow the instructions in How to Dye in the Vat (page 30) to dye your fabric.

CONSTRUCTION

Seam allowances are ½″ (1.3cm) unless otherwise stated.

1. On 1 short end, measure 10½″ (26.7cm) out from the center and make a mark; repeat on the other side of the center.

2. To ensure a very straight edge when using linen, I like to remove a thread to create a cutting channel. Clip into the selvage edge at one of the marked points. Locate a single thread along the marked line. Carefully pull that thread from the linen to form the cutting channel. If it gets too difficult to

pull the thread, cut it, smooth the fabric, and find the same thread. Use an awl or seam ripper to pull the thread free and start to pull again.

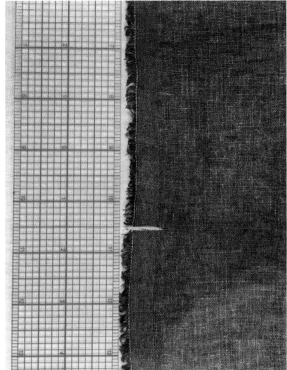

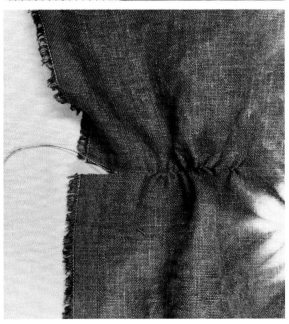

3. Repeat along the other long side.

4. Carefully cut along the cutting channels you just created. This will give you very straight edges when it comes time to hem the sides of the runner.

5. Repeat the process on the other 2 sides of the fabric, this time by removing a thread parallel and very close to each selvage edge. Follow the cutting channels you just made to remove the selvages.

6. Begin hemming the short ends first. Turn each of the edges under ½″ (1.3cm) and press. Turn under another ½″ (1.3cm) and press. Stitch down with matching thread.

7. Finish the long sides by turning the edges under ½″ (1.3cm) and press. Turn under again ½″ (1.3cm) and press. Stitch with matching thread along the hem to finish.

MAKE TURNING LONG EDGES EASY

To make turning long edges easy, I like to stitch along the side I'm going to turn by using the same seam allowance as the width I'll be turning. For example, on the table runner, I planned to turn under the long edges ½″ (1.3cm), so I first sewed along the long edges with a ½″ (1.3cm) seam allowance. This line gave me a reference point to make turning a cinch.

Photo by C&T Publishing, Inc.

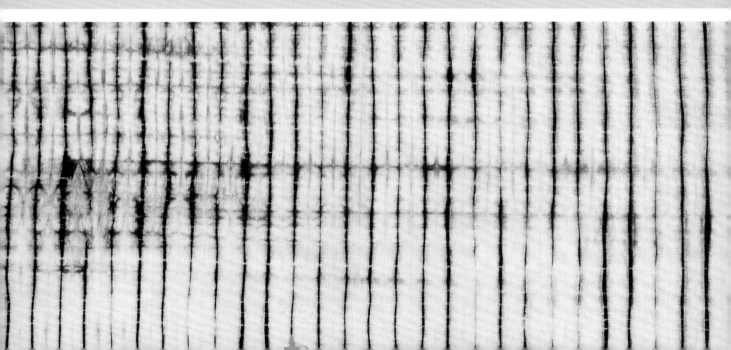

STRIPES FOR YOUR FAVORITE CHEF APRON

Finished apron: 40″ × 36″ (101.6 × 91.4cm); straps adjust to fit

Tesuji shibori creates the beautiful stripes on this apron. Whether given as a gift or worn when hosting friends for dinner, this apron is a statement piece and the perfect excuse to show off your dyeing skills!

MATERIALS

Medium-weight linen, cotton, or linen-blend fabric: 1¾ yards (1.6m) for the apron and pockets

1½″ (3.8cm) diameter rubber or plastic hose: 1¾ yards (1.6m)

Sewing thread in blue or white

Bonded nylon or heavy nylon upholstery thread

Long shibori needle for stitching

Ruler

Water-soluble marker

Blue painter's tape (if you are using a stencil)

Mesh bag from bulk fruit or vegetables, such as lemons or avocados

Heavyweight thread

Rubber bands

Optional: Pleating stencil, 1½″ × ⅜″ (see Resources, page 128)

Apron pattern download

CUTTING

Cut the apron body 40″ (101.6cm) × width of fabric. Set aside the remaining fabric for the pockets and straps.

DYEING THE FABRICS

1. Following the instructions in Tesuji (page 86), dye the apron body.

2. Following the instructions in Scrunch (page 98), dye the reserved pocket and strap fabric.

ACCESSING PATTERNS

To access the apron pattern through the tiny url, type the web address below into your browser window.

tinyurl.com/11561-pattern2-download

To access the download-able designs through the QR code, open the camera app on your phone, aim the camera at the QR code, and click the link that pops up on the screen.

Print directly from the browser window or download the pattern. To print at home, print the letter-size pages, selecting 100% size on the printer. Use dashed/dotted lines to trim, layer, and tape together pages as needed. To print at a copy shop, save the full-size pages to a thumb drive or email them to your local copy shop for printing.

Review the complete instructions for printing and tiling included in the pattern download PDF.

CONSTRUCTION

Seam allowances are ½″ (1.3cm) unless otherwise stated.

1. Using the downloaded and printed pattern, cut out the apron body. Mark the placement of the pockets.

2. Cut the pockets and straps (see Making the Straps, next page).

3. Turn all edges of the apron body under ½″ (1.3cm) and press. Turn under ½″ (1.3cm) again and press. Topstitch around all edges of the apron, close to the inner folded edge, and again close to the outer edge.

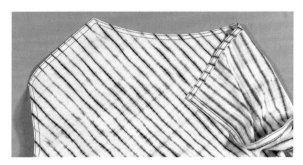

4. Prepare the pockets by securing the raw edges with a zigzag stitch (you can alternatively use a serger).

5. Turn the top edge down 1″ (2.5cm), right sides together, and stitch the sides with ⅜″ (1cm) seams.

6. Turn the top edge right sides out and stitch across the top. Stitch close to the edge, and again at ¾″ (1.9cm).

7. Turn the side and bottom edges under ⅜″ (1cm) and press.

8. Position the pockets by using your transferred marks as guidelines and pin in place. Topstitch the pocket to the apron, close to the edge, and again ½″ (1.3cm) in.

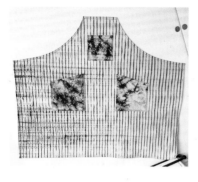

MAKING THE STRAPS

1. Measure how long your straps need to be to crossover from the left back top corner to the top right corner on the front of the apron.

2. Add about 4″ (10.2cm) to that length and cut 2 straps 3½″ (8.9cm) wide by the length you just calculated.

3. Fold each short end in ½″ (1.3cm) and topstitch. Fold the straps in half lengthwise, right sides together, and sew along the long edge with a ⅜″ (1cm) seam allowance.

4. Secure the side of 1 end with a large safety pin and feed it back through the fabric tube to turn the strap right side out. Sew the ends closed and press flat. Repeat Steps 2–4 to create the second strap.

5. Place the end of 1 of the straps under the left upper corner of the back of the apron. Topstitch a square with a cross in the middle to secure the strap to the back of the apron. Secure the second strap on the other side of the apron back.

6. Pin the other end of the back left-hand strap to the front top right corner of the apron. Pin the back right-hand strap to the other side. The straps should cross over in the back and attach to the opposite side of the front of the apron.

7. Try on the apron and adjust the straps as necessary. Stitch down securely with a square with a cross in the middle.

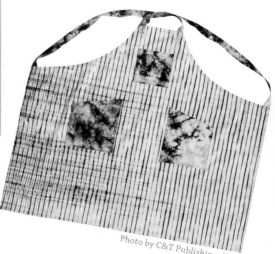

Photo by C&T Publishing, Inc.

PLAID TO DYE FOR SCARF

The arashi technique used to create this scarf is truly striking, particularly on narrow spaces, such as a scarf. For a truly one-of-a-kind gift or wardrobe statement, this scarf can't be beat.

MATERIALS

Premade silk scarf: 14˝ × 72˝ (36 × 183cm) or similar size

3˝ (7.6cm) PVC pipe at least 2½´ (76.2cm) long

Blue painter's tape

Twine or string

DYE THE SCARF

1. Follow the instructions in Basic Pole Wrapping (page 89) to prepare the scarf.

2. Follow the instructions in How to Dye in the Vat (page 30) to dye the scarf. Remove the scarf from the pole, but do not unfold, rinse, or finish the fabric.

3. Rotate your fabric bundle 90° and, beginning on the opposite top corner, rewrap the scarf onto your pole, this time wrapping in a counterclockwise direction. You should see your string crossing the previously undyed portions of the fabric.

4. Follow the instructions in How to Dye in the Vat (page 30) and Finishing the Fabrics (page 32) to finish your scarf.

Plaid to Dye for Scarf | Photo by C&T Publishing, Inc.

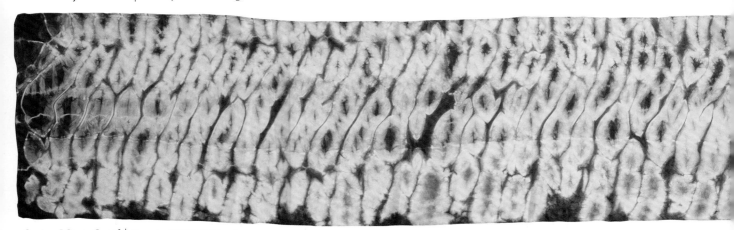

Spring Waves Scarf | Photo by C&T Publishing, Inc.

SPRING WAVES SCARF

If you are short on time or just want to play, the spring-toy resist technique is quirky and fun. It works best on scarves or lightweight fabrics and gives a beautiful result.

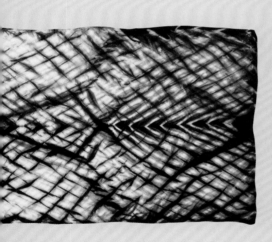

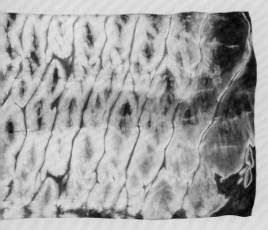

MATERIALS

Premade silk scarf:
14″ × 72″ (36 × 183cm) or similar size

Child's metal spring toy, such as a Slinky

3 pieces of strong twine or string about 15″ (38cm) each

DYE THE SCARF

Follow the instructions in Spring-Toy Resist (page 95).

GLOWING CIRCLES SHAWL

Who doesn't love polka dots?
And what is better than polka
dots that contain polka dots?

MATERIALS

Premade shawl: Premade or handmade shawl approximately 43″ × 90″ (109 × 229cm). I used a premade organic cotton mull shawl blank in very fine cotton with a rolled hem. It is so fine that it can be used as a scarf.

Ruler

4 C-clamps with at least a 2″ (5.1cm) depth from the screw to the throat of the clamp

Circle shapes: 2 that are 5″ (12.7cm) and 2 that are 4″ (10.2cm) for the resists in acrylic, wood, or metal

DYEING YOUR SHAWL

1. Follow the instructions in Five Ways to Fold the Fabric (page 36) to create an accordian-folded strip 7″ (17.8cm) wide.

2. Create a folded bundle by following the instructions in Square Fold (page 37).

3. Center the 5″ (12.7cm) circle resists on either side of the folded fabric bundle. Place 4 C-clamps around the perimeter of the circles. Screw the C-clamps down very tightly.

PERFECT CIRCLES
For a perfectly spaced design, you can measure from the edges of the square-folded fabric bundle to the edges of the circle resist on each side to ensure that your resist is centered.

4. Place the clamped shawl in water to wet it thoroughly—about 10 minutes because it is very fine fabric.

5. Squeeze as much water out of the piece as you can and then dip it in the indigo vat. While you have the piece in the dye, massage the folds on each side to open the spaces to allow the dye to flow in.

6. Dip it an additional 9 times, allowing the dye to oxidize between each dip.

7. Allow the dye to oxidize until you do not see any green. Rinse the shawl lightly and carefully. Remove the C-clamps and the resists, but be careful not to disturb the folds in the shawl.

8. Center the 4″ (10.2cm) circle resists on either side of the folded fabric bundle. Place 4 C-clamps around the perimeter of the circle. Screw the C-clamps down very tightly. Be sure that the edges of the C-clamps are not pushing against the side of the folds. If they do push, they'll act as a resist that you do not want.

MORE PERFECT CIRCLES—OR NOT!
To continue your perfectly spaced design, again measure from the edges of the

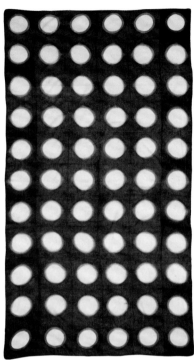

Photo by C&T Publishing, Inc.

square-folded fabric bundle to the edges of the circle resist on each side to ensure that your resist is centered. However, if you want a more off-kilter look, as long as your C-clamps have a deep-enough throat, you can position the 4″ (10.2cm) resists to one side of the white area instead of the center.

9. Dip the piece in the dye one time for several minutes, massaging the folds as before while in the dye.

10. Remove the piece and allow the dye to oxidize until you see no more green.

11. Rinse thoroughly and let it set overnight.

12. Follow the instructions in Opening the Bundles (page 31) and Finishing the Fabrics (page 32) to finish the shawl.

GIFTY SHAWL

I can't help myself—I have to show you how to do two different shawls.

They are both very easy, and the second one is the fastest method I know to make a fabulous shawl for a gift.

Photo by C&T Publishing, Inc.

MATERIALS

Premade shawl: Premade or handmade shawl approximately 43″ × 90″ (109 × 229cm). I used a premade organic cotton mull shawl blank in very fine cotton with a rolled hem. It is so fine that it can be used as a scarf.

4 yards (3.7m) ikat tape or smooth cord or ribbon

DYE THE SHAWL

Follow the instructions in Honeycomb (page 94), but use the Ikat tape to roll from two opposite corners toward the center, leaving a large center area unwrapped. Dye the shawl.

CONTEMPORARY SHIBORI QUILT

Finished quilt: 46″ × 56½″ (116.8 × 142.2cm)

This quilt highlights the beautiful shibori indigo samples you made while working your way through this book. For a fresh take, choose twelve fat quarters of fabric and select your favorite shibori designs.

MATERIALS

Undyed cotton: 3 yards (2.8m) or 12 fat quarters

Backing fabric: 3¼ yards (3m)

Binding fabric: ½ yard (45.7cm)

Batting: 54″ × 64″ (137 × 163cm)

Sewing thread in a blue to match the dyed fabric

Small labels or pieces of paper to mark the sizes of each piece

DYEING YOUR FABRIC

Flip through Major Techniques of Shibori (page 33) and select your favorites. You can select 12 different designs or repeat a few of your favorites.

For each fat quarter, you will need 17″ × 19″ (43.2 × 48.3cm) of usable fabric, so keep that in mind as you select your patterns and place your resists.

CUTTING

Refer to the cutting illustrations to cut the fat quarters. I marked the pieces with their cut sizes as I cut to make it easier to lay out the quilt.

From each of 2 fat quarters, cut:

A: 1 square 14½″ × 14½″ (36.8 × 36.8cm)

B: 1 rectangle 4″ × 14½″ (10.2 × 36.8cm)

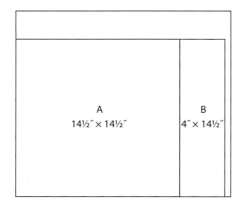

From 1 fat quarter, cut:

A: 1 square 14½″ × 14½″ (36.8 × 36.8cm)

C: 1 rectangle 4″ × 11″ (10.2 × 27.9cm)

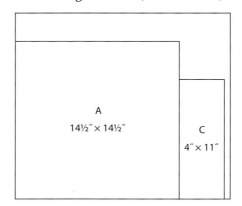

From 1 fat quarter, cut:

D: 2 rectangles 7½″ × 14½″ (19.1 × 36.8cm)

C: 1 rectangle 4″ × 11″ (10.2 × 27.9cm)

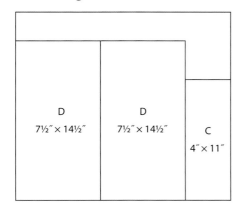

From 1 fat quarter, cut:

D: 1 rectangle 7½″ × 14½″ (19.1 × 36.8cm)

E: 1 rectangle 7½″ × 11″ (19.1 × 27.9cm)

C: 1 rectangle 4″ × 11″ (10.2 × 27.9cm)

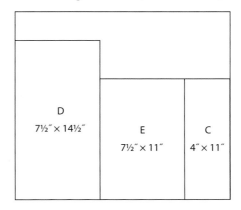

From each of 3 fat quarters, cut:

D: 1 rectangle 7½″ × 14½″ (19.1 × 36.8cm)

E: 1 rectangle 7½″ × 11″ (19.1 × 27.9cm)

F: 1 square 4″ × 4″ (10.2 × 10.2cm)

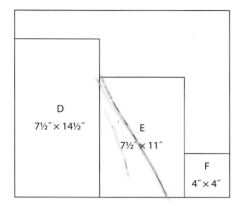

From 1 fat quarter, cut:

D: 1 rectangle 7½″ × 14½″ (19.1 × 36.8cm)

E: 1 rectangle 7½″ × 11″ (19.1 × 27.9cm)

G: 1 rectangle 4″ × 7½″ (10.2 × 19.1cm)

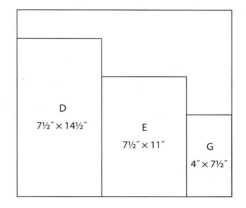

From each of 2 fat quarters, cut:

D: 1 rectangle 7½″ × 14½″ (19.1 × 36.8cm)

H: 1 square 7½″ × 7½″ (19.1 × 19.1cm)

G: 2 rectangles 4″ × 7½″ (10.2 × 19.1cm)

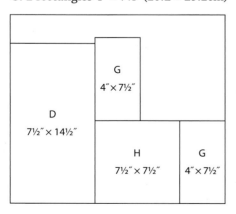

From 1 fat quarter, cut:

D: 1 rectangle 7½″ × 14½″ (19.1 × 36.8cm)

I: 1 rectangle 11″ × 14½″ (27.9 × 36.8cm)

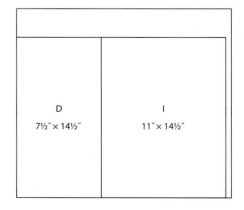

CONSTRUCTION

Seam allowances are ¼″ (6mm) unless otherwise stated.

ASSEMBLE THE UNITS

When sewing the following units together, press the seams to either direction. No seams have to nest.

1. Referring to the assembly diagram, arrange and rearrange the pieces until you are happy with your fabric placement.

2. Complete unit 1 by sewing F to G, then add C to one side and E to the bottom. Press.

3. Complete unit 2 by sewing G to E. Add H to E with a partial seam stopping at the dot and leaving the upper end of the seam unsewn as shown by the red line. Add a D to EH, another D to DH, and a third D to the final DH side, and then finish sewing the upper end of the partial seam between GE and DH as shown by the red line. Press.

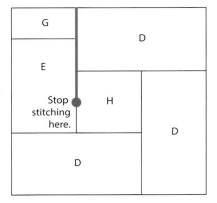

4. Complete unit 3 by sewing C to E to C. Then add A to the side and D to the other side of A. Press.

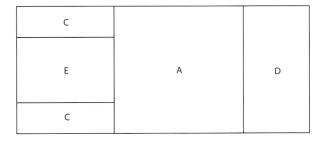

5. Complete unit 4 by sewing A to D. Press.

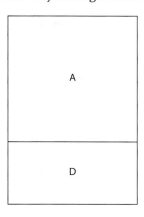

6. Complete unit 5 by sewing A to B. Press.

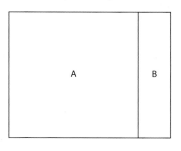

---

7. Complete unit 6 by sewing E to G with a partial seam, stopping at the dot and leaving the upper end of the seam unsewn as shown by the red line. Add I to EG, D to IG, and another D to the final DG side, and then finish sewing the end of the partial seam between E and DG as shown by the red line. Press.

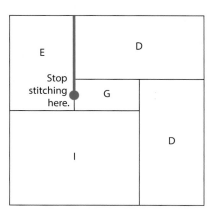

8. Complete unit 7 by sewing D to H with a partial seam, stopping at the dot and leaving the upper end of the seam unsewn as shown by the red line. Add another D to DH, and a third D to DH. Sew G to E, then add this unit to the final side of DH. Finish sewing the end of the partial seam between D and EH as shown by the red line. Sew F to B to F and then add to DG. Press.

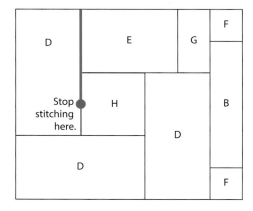

ASSEMBLE THE QUILT TOP

Refer to the assembly layout as needed.

1. Sew unit 1 to unit 2, then add rectangle G with a partial seam stopping at the dot and leaving the upper end of the seam unsewn as shown by the red line. Press.

2. Add unit 3 to the bottom of units 1/2/G. Press.

3. Add unit 4 to unit 3/G. Press.

4. Add unit 5 to unit 4/G and then finish sewing the end of the partial seam between unit 1/2 and 5/G as shown by the red line. Press.

5. Sew unit 6 to unit 7 and then add this unit to the bottom of units 3/4. Press.

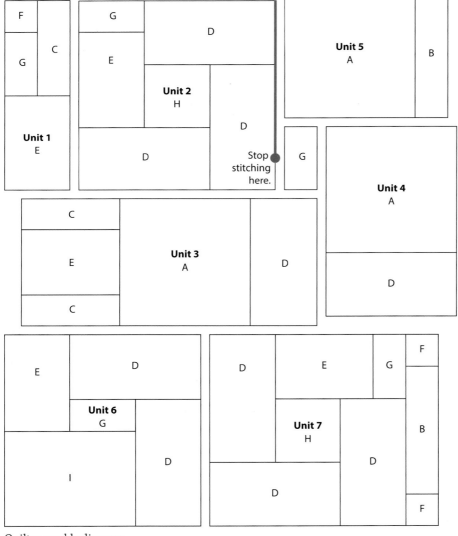

Quilt assembly diagram

QUILT AND BIND

1. Create a quilt sandwich by layering the backing wrong side up, the batting, and then the quilt top right side up. Pin or baste together.

2. Quilt and bind as desired. Very simple straight-line big-stitch quilting looks great on this type of quilt.

Photo by C&T Publishing, Inc.

ABOUT THE AUTHOR

Debbie Maddy is a textile artist with a passion for shibori techniques and natural indigo dye. She began her career with simple resists and has advanced to more intricate stitching as well as fold-and-clamp and arashi pole wrapping. Debbie has traveled to Japan to attend the Japanese Textile Workshops led by Bryan Whitehead at his Japanese silk-farming farmhouse. The daily classes emphasized the techniques of pleating and stitching as in Katano shibori as well as pleating and wrapping for tesuji shibori. While there, she attended a class with a master paste-resist stencil dyer.

Debbie studied in England with Jane Callender, an expert in stitched shibori. In the United States, she has been fortunate to learn from African artists Gasali Adeyemo of Nigeria and Aboubakar Fofana of Mali. She searches for knowledge from all the shibori textbooks she can acquire. She cherishes her Japanese shibori books, even though she cannot read the text. Debbie has a passion for shibori and indigo and loves sharing her art with others. Find her courses on the innovative and interactive platform Creative Spark Online Learning (by C&T Publishing).

RESOURCES

Tiori Designs
This is my own shop, where you'll find indigo dye, indigo vat kits, all the stencils used in this book, Japanese kimono fabric, a wide selection of fabric and items prepared for dyeing, needles, threads, resists, and more. • **debbiemaddy.com**

Maiwa
Maiwa carries ikat tape, a variety of indigo dyes, supplies, and a wide selection of fabric and items prepared for dyeing. • **maiwa.com**

Dharma Trading Co.
At Dharma, you'll find a variety of indigo dyes, supplies, and a wide selection of fabric and items prepared for dyeing. • **dharmatrading.com**

Botanical Colors
Botanical Colors carries a variety of indigo dyes, supplies, kits, and a wide selection of fabric and items prepared for dyeing. • **botanicalcolors.com**

Slow Fiber Studios
You'll find fabric, dyes, and tools, including the sometimes difficult-to-locate miura needle, at Slow Fiber Studios. • **shop.slowfiberstudios.com**

Atelier Miyabi
Atelier Miyabi carries a unique selection of imported tools and supplies, including the elusive miura needle. • **ateliermiyabi.com**

Visit Debbie online and follow on social media!

Website: debbiemaddy.com
Instagram: @debbie_maddy
Pinterest: /debbie_maddy
Facebook: /debbie.maddy
YouTube: /@DebbieMaddy
Creative Spark: creativespark.ctpub.com